EWELL
PAST

The junction of Cheam Road and the High Street, *c.*1910. The building containing the Shapland Motor Works and Beams the shoemaker was converted into the Midland Bank in the 1960s and has more recently become the HSBC.

EWELL PAST

Charles Abdy

Phillimore

2000

Published by
PHILLIMORE & CO. LTD.
Shopwyke Manor Barn, Chichester, West Sussex

ISBN 1 86077 135 1

Printed and bound in Great Britain by
BIDDLES LTD.
Guildford, Surrey

Contents

List of Illustrations

frontispiece: The junction of Cheam Road and the High Street, *c*.1910

Illustration Acknowledgements

Mr. G. Alexander, 16; Mr. F. Arend, 136; Mr. J. Beams, 149; Mrs. P.Bedwell, 21, 75, 150; Bourne Hall Library, 17, 31, 36, 56, 88, 101, 115; Bourne Hall Museum, frontispiece, 2-8, 12, 15, 17, 22-4, 27, 33, 37, 39-41, 44-5, 54, 57-9, 61-5, 67, 81-3, 85, 91-9, 102-5, 107-9, 111-14, 117-22, 124, 126, 128, 131-3, 137, 139-43, 148, 151-2, 155-7; The Fitzwilliam Museum, Cambridge, 13; Ford Motor Co., 153; Glyn House Administration, 87, 92; Mr. C. Hallifax, 125; Mr. and Mrs. P. Harper, 127; Mr. E. Jeal, 60; King Edward's School, 35; Mr. P.Lelliot, 138; Ordnance Survey, 10, 11; Mr. E.A. Sparrow, 134; Surrey Record Society, 14; Tate Gallery, 48; Mrs. O. Temple, 80; Mr. A.E. Tims, 53, 70, 71; Mr. D. Vanstone, 135; Mr. P. Wallum, 46, 154; Mr. L. Yates, 158.

The following are reproduced by permission of Surrey History Service: 28, 29, 49, 50, 74, 76, 116, 129.

Unattributed illustrations are mostly from the author's collection. I have done my best to trace the owners of photographs that have been used: if I have missed any I apologise.

Acknowledgements

I would like to express my warm thanks to the following:

To the Curator of Bourne Hall Museum, Jeremy Harte, and his assistant, David Brooks, for making available so many pictures from the museum's extensive collection of old photographs.

To the staff of Bourne Hall Library for their willing assistance in tracking down information, and similarly the staff of the Surrey History Centre at Woking.

With regard to the chapter on the Second World War, special thanks go to Geoff Howell, who, working at Bourne Hall Museum, put together a great deal of information that I was able to consult. The chapter on the River Hogsmill and its mills owes much to the paper by Maurice Exwood referred to in the bibliography, and for the chapter on Stoneleigh, Alan Jackson's *Semi-detached London* was an invaluable source of facts and I am grateful to Charles Hallifax, who has known Stoneleigh for many years, for reading this chapter.

The help of members of Nonsuch Antiquarian Society is acknowledged, in particular the Documentary Group for giving permission to make use of material from the Occasional Paper on Ewell Public Houses in History. Ian West updated my information on the old buildings of Ewell. Members of staff of Nescot must be thanked for having made information available and allowing me to take photographs on their farm.

The extracts from Assize Records in Chapter 5 are reproduced from J.S. Cockburn, ed., *Calendar of Assize Records: Surrey Indictments, Elizabeth I,* 1980 and *James I,* 1982, by permission of the Public Record Office on behalf of the Controller of Her Majesty's Stationery Office.

Finally, the book would not have been possible without the help of my wife Barbara, to say nothing of her prowess with a word-processor.

Ewell—Ye well—in Surrey, at the time I speak of, had a true claim to be a home of repose ... the wide earth's thank offering of a spring of water outpouring in its sparkling purity is ever a delight to the soul of man. The village itself had no sense of modern bustling or hurry; all was arranged spaciously, all work executed with deliberation, and with such unostentation that externally there was but little to distinguish the chemist's shop from the baker's or any other tradesman's house from that of his neighbour.

(From the autobiography of Holman Hunt, who made several visits to Ewell as a young man.)

Introduction

When my book *A History of Ewell* was published in 1992, there were people who said that I should never have written it: I had lived in Ewell for only ten years! However, others found the book of sufficient interest to buy it and the publishers asked me to write another book on Ewell. It has been difficult to decide on the contents. I did not wish to repeat too much of the original material; on the other hand, new readers would expect at least an outline of the major events in the history of the parish. And so I have given a brief overall account of the history and then elaborated on particular aspects of the story in more detail than was possible in the previous book.

In the introduction to the 1992 book, I said it was an album of snapshots of the past: given the multitudinous facets of the past of any area, it is difficult to visualise a history book that could claim to be more than that and still be readable. Many years ago a famous scientist, looking back over his life, said he had been like a child picking up brightly coloured pebbles on the beach, while the whole ocean of truth lay undiscovered before him. I would not put local history research quite like that; rather it is a matter of one thing leading to another, of one stone moved revealing many more underneath, of constantly expanding vistas. All one can hope to do is to try to fix the image of particular events as they appear from one's viewpoint at a given time. I recognise that there are many aspects of Ewell that I have not dealt with: it seemed best to cover in some detail things I have found of particular interest rather than attempting to include everything within the number of pages the publisher has been prepared to provide.

Although the presentation is broadly chronological, certain aspects of the history are best treated thematically, so that here and there details that might have been expected in Part 2 appear in Part 1 and vice versa.

Chapter One

Prehistoric and Roman Ewell

History is a play performed against scenery and the development of the parish of Ewell is related to the geology of the area. The old village is on the spring line that runs across Surrey from Croydon to the Clandons and which gave rise to a chain of villages such as Beddington, Carshalton and Cheam. The spring line runs along the strip of porous Reading and Thanet beds that separates the upper chalk and the London clay.

1 View across Ewell Village looking towards Epsom, from the tower of Old Church.

The Ewell springs were celebrated in times past: in the Dipping Place at the High Street-Spring Street junction, water gushed up in great quantity, water of exceptional purity and coldness. Tradition has it that when Elizabeth I stayed at nearby Nonsuch Palace she insisted on a daily supply of fresh water from the Ewell springs. These springs were the source of the Hogsmill River that flows north-west in an alluvium-bottomed valley through areas of London clay and Taplow Terrace gravel before joining the Thames at Kingston.

The centre of the village is on the Reading and Thanet beds and some alluvium; to the north is London clay and to the south east is upper chalk. The altitude is between 35 and 45m. Going south there is a gradual rise over the chalk of the North Downs to a height of

155m on Epsom Downs and about five kilometres (three miles) farther south the summit of the North Downs is reached with an altitude of around 200m. The old village was at the centre of an approximately north-south strip parish about six kilometres (3¾ miles) long and one and a half kilometres (just under one mile) wide.

The abundant water supply and a terrain that would have been good hunting country would have attracted Stone-Age man, although Palaeolithic people have left little evidence of their presence. There have been numerous finds from the Mesolithic period, including flint-working areas. Many of the sites of finds were on rising ground close to the river. There is flint in abundance in the chalk of the North Downs, and this was the main source of supply for the artefacts found, although some microliths

2   The Dipping Place, Ewell Village, c.1920. Water of exceptional purity and coldness gushed up here.

3 Late Bronze-Age axe-head found in Bourne Hall Lake.

4 Bronze-Age spear head found in Bourne Hall Lake.

appear to have been made from pebbles that came from the gravel beds that occur along the river. The valleys of the Hogsmill, the Wey and the Mole enabled Mesolithic occupation to progress from the Thames.

Not much has been found from the Neolithic and Bronze Ages other than a few flints, a Beaker drinking vessel and a few bronze spear heads, axes and awls. The Iron Age is better represented: three occupation sites and several pits have been identified, consistent with a series of Iron-Age farming communities.

Roman Ewell

Shortly after their arrival in A.D. 43, the Romans built the road from London Bridge to Chichester that we now call Stane Street. Chichester was an important base in the early days of the occupation, and later, with the development of London as the major Roman town, it was a supply port for the capital. The route of Stane Street from London Bridge to Ewell is said to be so precisely aligned with Chichester that, if continued on the same line, it would have entered the east gate of that town!

5 Excavation of a Roman well at Purberry Shot, Epsom Road, Ewell, in 1938-9.

However, at Ewell the Roman road deviated from the direct line, one theory being that doing so brought it quicker onto the chalk and avoided areas of more difficult ground. Other deviations in the course of Stane Street were made to take it through the North Downs at the Mole gap, and through the South Downs between Pulborough and Chichester.

Given that the alignment from London Bridge was aimed at Chichester, it was indeed fortunate that it took the road so close to the springs at Ewell; it certainly made the place an ideal site for the settlement that grew up there. The first published account of important finds of Roman material was in 1847 following the exposure of numerous shafts when a chalk pit was dug (where Sainsbury's Homebase is now). These finds included animal bones, metal objects and pottery. There has since been a considerable

amount of archaeology in Ewell, as well as chance discovery of Roman remains. A Gazetteer of Romano-British archaeological sites in Ewell published by the Surrey Archaeological Society in 1997 lists nearly ninety sites. The evidence points to a sizeable Roman settlement, although experts are still undecided whether it should be described as a small town or a village. Foundations of buildings were unearthed and a great amount of pottery. More than four hundred coins are referred to and many more would have been casually picked up in gardens and unrecorded. The coins found cover the period of the Roman occupation of Britain with very few gaps.

There are two archaeological excavations that are of particular importance. Excavations in the Old Fair Field in Ewell in 1933 conducted by A.W.G. Lowther and S.E. Winbolt revealed a considerable length of Stane Street. (The Old Fair Field was behind the *Green Man* public house.) And then in the period 1967-77 there were very extensive excavations behind the *King William IV* public house (currently called *The Friend and Firkin*) in Ewell High Street, carried out by the Nonsuch Antiquarian Society under various directors. The work involved digging 26 trenches, which revealed many wells and pits. The material recovered had a date range from A.D. 70 to the fourth century and included remains of buildings, pottery, glass, metal and bone artefacts. There were some 30 coins plus a hoard of 120 third-century coins in a bronze flagon. A very comprehensive report on the dig by the Institute of Archaeology archaeologist Clive Orton was published by the Surrey Archaeological Society in 1997. The *King William IV* site was on the presumed course of Stane Street, and the archaeologists were surprised to find no trace of the road. Clive Orton has put forward an interesting theory to explain its absence. Finds of pre-Roman material, including a Beaker burial and an Iron-Age burial pit, had suggested that the site was a sacred location, hallowed by usage and a long

VESPASIAN 69-79	SEVERUS ALEXANDER 222-235
TRAJAN 98-117	GALLIENUS 253-268
HADRIAN 117-138	POSTHUMUS 260-268
ANTONINUS PIUS 138-161	CLAUDIUS GOTHICUS 268-269
MARCUS AURELIUS 161-180	VICTORINUS 269-271
COMMODUS 176-192	TETRICUS I AND II 271-273
SEPTIMIUS SEVERUS 193-211	CONSTANTINE I 307-337

6 Roman coins found during excavations on the *King William IV* site in 1967-77, covered a large part of the Roman occupation of Britain.

7 & 8 Roman bronze mask from Glyn House grounds (*below left*) and a Roman pottery mask from Ewell Village (*below right*) each approximately 4.5 cm long.

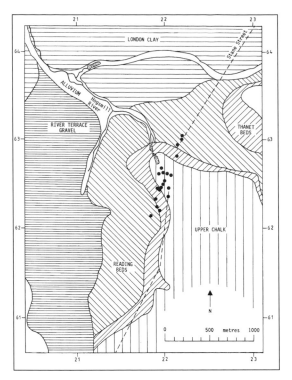

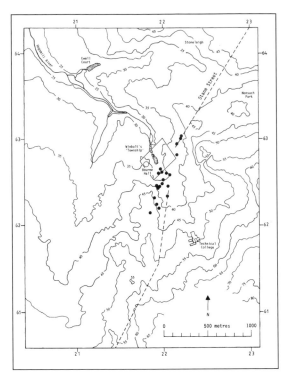

9   The geology of the Ewell area.   **10**   The topography of the Ewell area.

Dots indicate major Roman finds.

folk memory. So as not to desecrate such a site, and upset the natives, the Romans took their road round it, rather than through it.

The activity came to an abrupt end some time between A.D. 280 and 380, when the buildings were demolished and the site was cleared. Clive Orton said this may be due to the progress of Christianity in the area after it had gained Imperial toleration in A.D. 313. The thoroughness of the levelling of the site suggests a wish to wipe out all traces of its pagan past.

The Nonsuch Antiquarian Society has been responsible for a great deal of archaeology in Ewell in addition to the *King William IV* dig. The Society was set up in 1960 by people who had taken part in the excavation of Nonsuch Palace the previous year, and it still holds regular meetings.

One of the mysteries of Ewell is the way that Stane Street went out of use after the Roman legions went home. From London Bridge to the outskirts of Ewell village the Roman road has by and large been in continuous use: much of the A24 follows its line. Traces of the agger are to be seen along London Road on the north west of Nonsuch Park. But at Briarwood Road the modern roads leave Stane Street and do not pick it up again until south of Dorking, if we exclude the rough track of Pebble Lane south of Epsom. At some places where the road metal has been found in Ewell it has been under more than two feet of topsoil, and possibly there was a period after the Romans left when the settlement was deserted. Much of the centre is low-lying and could well have been subject to flooding from the springs that were the source of the River Hogsmill. This would be conducive to a build-up of silt that would soon obliterate the road.

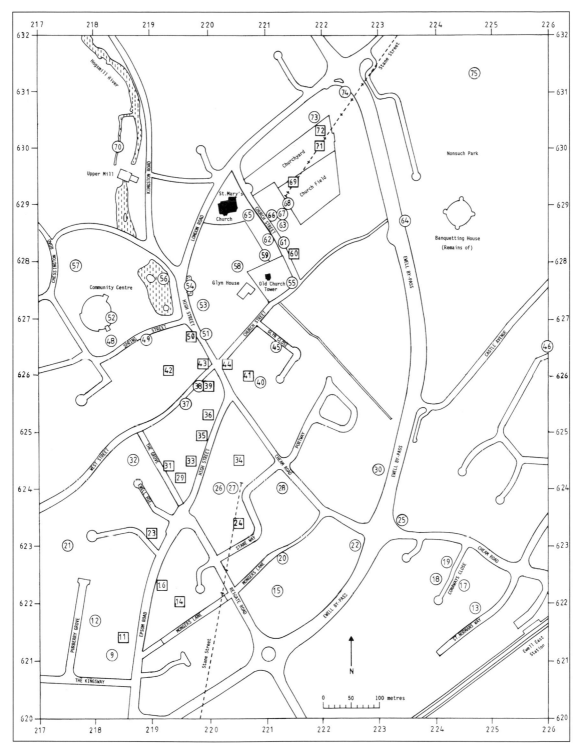

11 Finds near the centre of Ewell Village. Numbered circles and squares indicate finds of Roman material as in Gazetteer referred to on page 4.

Chapter Two

Saxon and Medieval Ewell, the Manors and the Church

Saxon Ewell

Evidence of Saxon settlement in Ewell is provided by archaeology: an extensive cemetery has been found in The Grove and Ewell House area. The first known reference is in John Aubrey's *Natural History and Antiquities of the County of Surrey*, published in 1718, which said that human bones had been unearthed in the grounds of Ewell House. In 1930 three burials were found when a trench for an electric cable was taken along The Grove. There were more finds in 1932, and in 1934 when Lowther and Winbolt carried out excavations. In all, at least 12 burials were found with grave goods that included knives, spearheads, shield bosses, rings and brooches. Some of these burials were cinerary urns, but bodies were also found, including one having a west to east orientation, which suggests that the cemetery was in use through pagan and Christian periods. A further skeleton was found during cable laying in 1993. So far the site of the settlement that would have been associated with the funerary site is unknown.

Graves have also been discovered cut in the chalk of the Downs to the south of the Ewell parish boundary. As recently as 1986 more than forty Saxon graves dating back to probably the late sixth or early seventh century were uncovered following a discovery during development work at Tadworth.

12 One of more than forty Saxon graves uncovered at Tadworth in 1986.

13 The bones from Tadworth were given a Christian burial in one large coffin at Banstead parish church on 30 September 1996.

There is considerable uncertainty as to the origin of the Saxons who settled in the Ewell area: whereas some of the grave goods are comparable with material found at Croydon, Beddington and Mitcham, some experts have suggested that the area was settled by the South Saxons pushing north.

The first mention of Ewell is in the foundation charter of Chertsey Abbey *c*.675 when 30 mansas of land in Ewell and Cuddington were granted to the new abbey by Frithwald, the under-king of Surrey. However, it has to be said that the charter exists only in a mid-13th-century copy, and there is some doubt as to the validity of the claim.

By the time of the Norman Conquest, Ewell was a royal manor. It was referred to in Domesday Book under Copthorne Hundred as 'Etwelle: King's land, two Mills'. It had 48 villagers and four smallholders with 15 ploughs. The value before 1066 was put at £20 and it is interesting to note that Kingston, an

important town where seven Saxon kings were reputedly crowned, was valued at £30, only £10 more than Ewell. Therefore, it seems that Saxon Ewell was a place of some consequence. Domesday Book makes no reference to a church at Ewell, but it does say that the church at Leret (Leatherhead) was attached to the manor with 40 acres of arable land valued at 20s. The entry for Epsom, which belonged to Chertsey Abbey, refers to two churches, and it is believed that one of these was the Ewell church. There is also a passage to the effect that the 'men of the Hundred of Copthorne testify that two hides and one virgate were removed from this manor. They were there in the time of King Edward but the reeves lent them to their friends.'

This passage is believed to relate to Kingswood and it would appear that the land reverted to the Crown, since Kingswood was granted to Merton Priory by Henry II along with Ewell.

Medieval Ewell and the Manors

Ewell was a royal manor until 1158, when it was granted to Merton Priory and the priors became lords of the manor. They remained so until the dissolution of Merton in 1538, although at times they assigned the lordship to others. After the dissolution Ewell manor was leased to various people and then in 1563 Elizabeth I granted it to Henry, Earl of Arundel, and his heirs, for the sum of £885 12s. 10d.

There were three sub-manors associated with Ewell. Fitznells' manor was founded by a Mr. Robert, rector of Cuddington, who built up a small estate of strips in the open fields of Cuddington and Ewell and some property in Cuddington village. In 1311 the estate passed into the hands of Sir Robert fitz Neil and was subsequently known as Fitznells. It retained that name when it passed to later owners. In 1331 the estate consisted of 250 acres of arable land, six acres of meadow and three water mills. In the second half of the 17th century the manor was conveyed to Thomas Turgis. Part of the manor house built around 1540 survives in the building known as Fitznell's Manor.

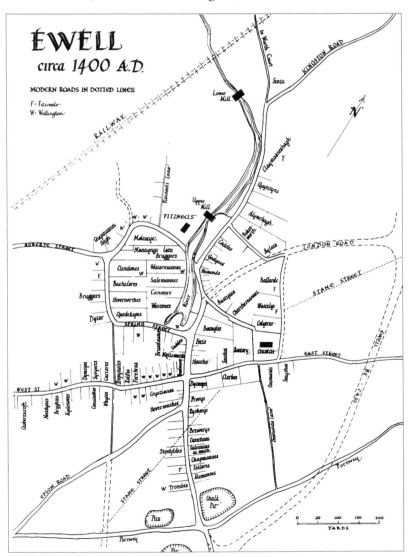

14 Ewell, *c*.1400: a conjectural map by C.A.F. Meekings and P. Shearman.

The manor of Batailles took its name from its first owner, William de Bataille, who was granted it by Henry I at the beginning of the 12th century. The land was mostly scattered in the arable furlongs but with some enclosures just north of the village. The manor house lay on the north-eastern outskirts of the village on a site within the grounds of the present Glyn House. After going through various hands, Batailles passed by marriage to the Saunder family. By 1577 nearly all the land now forming Bourne Hall grounds had been acquired by the Saunders. Five generations of them possessed Batailles Manor before it was sold to Thomas Turgis in 1659.

Ruxley manor had originally been called Shawford, after it first owner. The name had many transformations until *c.*1480 when it was changed to Rokesley, the then owner and finally became Ruxley. In 1577 the manor lands consisted of at least 120 acres on the north of Ewell, plus some property in the village. Thomas Turgis acquired Ruxley Manor in the second half of the 17th century and so became owner of all three of the Ewell sub-manors. They passed through other hands and in 1784 were sold to Thomas Calverley, who built a mansion called Ewell Castle, now Ewell Castle School, in Church Street, Ewell. In subsequent years the manors were split up and sold off.

The Church

Although the manor of Ewell belonged to Merton Priory, the church was on land owned by Chertsey Abbey. The building that was demolished when the new St Mary's church was built in 1847-8 had a 13th-century nave, although traces of 11th- and 12th-century work are said to have been found. The old church stood some 140 yards to the south of the present church. Initially, Chertsey Abbey appointed the vicars, but in 1415 the advowson was given to Henry V who the following year granted the church to the Prior and Convent of Newark, who retained it until the Dissolution. The advowson remained with the Crown for some

15 When the old parish church was demolished following the building of the new one in 1847-8, the tower was left standing for use as a mortuary chapel. This shows it *c.*1905.

time after the Dissolution, and then became part of the Rectory Estate, which had various owners before it came by marriage to the Glyn family towards the middle of the 18th century. George Glyn became vicar in 1831 and served for 50 years. The Glyn family continued as patrons of the church until the death of Margaret, the last of the Glyns of Ewell, in 1946. The Bishop of Guildford is now the patron. Until the founding of the Diocese of Guildford in 1927, Ewell was in the Diocese of Winchester and gave its name to one of the four deaneries of Surrey, the others being Southwark, Guildford and Croydon. The Ewell deanery existed until the reorganisation of rural deaneries in the 19th century.

16 St Mary the Virgin, Ewell, as painted in 1847 by the young Holman Hunt at the request of the Rev. Sir George Glyn.

17 The bells of St Mary's prior to their return to the founders for repair and retuning in July 1970.

Chapter Three

Tudor and 17th-century Ewell, Cuddington and Nonsuch Palace

The major event of Tudor Ewell was the building of Nonsuch Palace in the neighbouring parish of Cuddington and the enclosure of land that had been tilled for centuries to form the Great and Little Parks. The enclosure extended beyond the area of Cuddington parish and took in more than 150 acres of Ewell.

Cuddington and Nonsuch Palace

Although in medieval times Ewell and Cuddington were completely separate parishes, following the destruction of Cuddington village and the building of Nonsuch Palace by Henry VIII, aspects of the administration of Cuddington parish became the concern of

18   Nonsuch Palace, *c*.1620, by an unknown artist. The palace was demolished towards the end of the 17th century.

Ewell parish. It was in 1538 that Cuddington village was demolished because Henry VIII had decided that he wanted his new palace of Nonsuch to be built there. But clearly that was not the end of the story: there is still a Cuddington parish and a local government ward of that name, a name that is attached also to some things outside the present parish.

Cuddington prior to 1538

The old Cuddington was a strip parish running more or less north to south alongside Ewell parish and to the east of it. The length was nearly four miles and the width just under a mile. As with Ewell, the strip encompassed London clay in the north and downland chalk in the south separated by a band of lighter soils on which the village stood.

Recent excavations on what was Warren Farm have indicated occupation of the area during the Iron Age and earlier periods. The earliest mention of Cuddington is in the copy of the foundation charter of Chertsey Abbey of *c*.675 in which land in Cuddington (and Ewell) was granted to the new abbey.

William the Conqueror gave the manor to his half-brother, Odo of Bayeux. At the time of Domesday Book the tenant was Ilbert de Laci. There were 11 villagers, 13 smallholders, 4 slaves, 7 ploughs and a mill valued at 40d. The value of the manor before 1066 was £11; in 1086, £9 12s. (By comparison, Ewell had 48 villagers, 4 smallholders, 15 ploughs and 2 mills valued at 10s. The value of the manor before 1066 was £20: in 1086, £16.) In the 13th century the St Michael family were the holders, and they eventually took the name Codington.

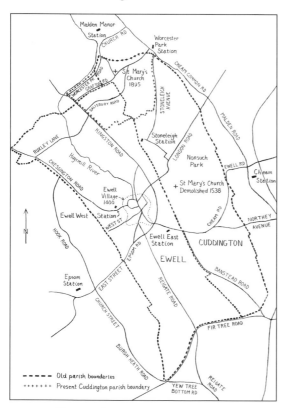 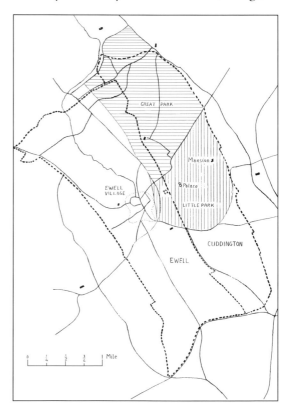

19　Ewell and Cuddington. The boundaries of the old parishes in relation to modern roads.

20　Cuddington, Ewell and Nonsuch Palace.

The excavation of Nonsuch Palace in 1959 revealed the foundations of the church which is thought to have started in about the year 1100 as a simply built nave and chancel, possibly replacing an earlier wooden structure. It was altered and extended at various periods so that by 1538 it was a sizeable building with a tower at the west end. The manor house stood near the churchyard, and a description of it is available in the report prepared by Henry VIII's surveyors. It formed one side of a courtyard, on two other sides of which were barns and stables, while the fourth side consisted of a wall with a small gatehouse.

Even by medieval standards the village was small: a taxation survey of 1428 shows fewer than ten inhabited houses. However, Henry's surveyors were complimentary about the quality of the surrounding land and the abundance of game.

Walter de Merton

Possibly the most famous name associated with Cuddington, if one excludes Henry VIII, who might be better described as infamous in this connection, is Walter de Merton, who came to Cuddington as Rector in about 1238. He had been known as Walter of Basingstoke, but because he had been educated at Merton Priory before going to Oxford, he changed his name to Merton. Walter's education proved to be worthwhile: by 1260 he had been appointed Lord Chancellor of England. He acquired substantial estates, including the manors of Malden and Farleigh, the revenues from which supported Merton College Oxford which he founded. The House of Scholars of Merton was initially for the education of Walter's nephews and other connections, including two of the children of Gilbert of Ewell who had married Walter's sister Agnes. Gilbert of Ewell held the estate subsequently known as Fitznell's Manor. In 1274 Walter became Bishop of Rochester. When Walter de Merton died in 1277 he left 20 marks to the poor of Cuddington.

The Destruction of Cuddington and the Building of Nonsuch Palace

Henry VIII's desire for a palace at Cuddington was part of a plan for a great hunting estate based on Hampton Court and extending as far south as Walton-on-the-Hill. His growing infirmities and corpulence made him loath to travel farther afield for his pleasures. The plan involved the rebuilding of the medieval palace at Oatlands at Weybridge and the construction of a new palace at Cuddington to provide hunting lodges. The new palace was to demonstrate to the world, and in particular his rival Francis I, Henry's wealth and magnificence. It was to be a nonsuch. In the words of John Dent, 'there emerged a building of unrivalled splendour, lavishly decorated to the point of vulgarity, a monument to princely ostentation.' This most remarkable of Tudor buildings was built around two courtyards, the inner court being surrounded by the royal apartments, the buildings of which were covered with moulded plaster panels with classical motifs, surrounded by frames of carved slate, much of the decoration being gilded. The south front was flanked by towers five storeys high. There were statues and fountains, and the palace was surrounded by ornamental gardens with more statues and fountains.

The great enterprise was supported by the wealth that came to the King from the dissolution of the monasteries, and in a more direct way by the use of stone from the demolished Merton Priory in the foundations of the palace. When Henry VIII died in 1547 the palace was unfinished, although more or less habitable. Its completion had to wait until the reign of Elizabeth I, when the Earl of Arundel who had acquired Nonsuch had the remaining work carried out so that the Queen could be invited to a magnificent and extravagant palace-warming party in 1559.

The building stood on slightly rising ground in what was designated the Little Park, separated from the Great Park to the north by what is now London Road. The area of the

21 The young Martin Biddle, later Professor Martin Biddle, in the site hut during the large-scale excavation of Nonsuch Palace in 1959 of which he was the director.

22 Nonsuch Palace excavations, 1959. They were probably the largest archaeological excavations ever carried out in a single year in this country.

Little Park was more than 600 acres and its creation involved the closure of the old road from Ewell Village to Cheam and the making of a new road curving round the southern boundary of the park, the present Cheam Road. The Great Park had an area of well over 1,000 acres. Although the bulk of the parks was in Cuddington, 153 acres had been in the parish of Ewell and 145 acres in Malden. Old Cuddington no longer existed: it had become part of 'The Manor of Nonesuche otherwise Codingtonne'.

Richard Codington

When Henry first set his covetous eyes on Cuddington, the lord of the manor was Richard Codington, descendant of a family that had been in possession since the early 13th century. Sir Simon de Codington had been Sheriff of Surrey in 1353 and 1362. His son Ralph was Sheriff in 1400. Both men sat for Surrey in several Parliaments. Richard Codington and his wife Elizabeth gave the King 'The Manor of Codington and other premises in Surrey' in exchange for 'The site of the late Priory of Ixworth [Suffolk] with the Church, Steeple and Churchyard and all messuages and lands thereto belonging'.

It is unlikely that Richard Codington was overjoyed when the King proposed that he should leave his ancestral home and move to Suffolk, but it is equally unlikely that he would have voiced objections to the move. Considered purely in terms of the value of Cuddington compared with that of the extensive Ixworth properties, it would seem that Richard and Elizabeth did quite well out of the exchange. The Cuddington manor was small and does not seem to have been prosperous.

The Parish without a Church

Although Cuddington Church was demolished in 1538 and no replacement was built, in the eyes of the church authorities the parish remained in existence. The Cuddington Vestry was still meeting in the 19th century and returns made for administrative purposes refer to the parish of Cuddington long after the village was destroyed. Parish registers of adjacent parishes such as Ewell and Cheam indicate that people living in Cuddington used the churches of these other parishes for worship and ceremonies such as baptism and burial.

Cuddington Manor

After the death of Henry VIII, lordship of the manor passed through various hands, including those of the Duke of Bedford, who in 1755 sold it to Edward Northey of Epsom, who bought Ewell manor in the same year. The manorial courts were held jointly for Ewell and Cuddington.

The Rise and Fall of the Nonsuch Palace Estate

Although the Palace was unfinished when Henry VIII died on 28 January 1547, he had been able to stay there on short visits on several occasions. Edward VI and his successor, Queen Mary, showed little interest in Nonsuch and in 1556 Mary sold the Palace and Little Park to the Earl of Arundel, who had the Palace completed. The Earl left Nonsuch to his son-in-law, Lord Lumley, along with enormous debts, in settlement of which the Palace was given to Elizabeth. The queen began spending money on the building and the court met there frequently: it was the heyday of Nonsuch.

Elizabeth was at Nonsuch on 28 September 1599 when there occurred one of those dramatic incidents that go down in history. The Earl of Essex, one-time favourite of the Queen, had been sent to Ireland to put down a rebellion, but had not carried out his instructions. Anxious to explain himself to Elizabeth in person, he had hurried to the palace, and burst into her bedroom unannounced while the Queen was dressing. Since she was without her wig and her face was unpainted, she was not pleased, and it did not help Essex to put his case. He spent a year in captivity at York House for his actions in

Ireland and his unauthorised return. Shortly after, he was put on trial for plotting against the Queen and was executed in February 1601.

James I settled Nonsuch on the Queen, Anne of Denmark, and the royal family made some use of the palace. Charles I came to the throne in 1625 and in 1627 granted Nonsuch to his Queen, Henrietta Maria.

During the Civil War, Nonsuch was occupied by the Roundheads. The parks suffered badly in this period: many fine trees were felled for timber. John Evelyn visited Nonsuch in January 1666, the Office of the Exchequer having been transferred there during the plague of the previous year. He reported that

> there stand in the garden two handsome stone pyramids and the avenue planted with rows of fair elms, but the rest of those goodly trees both of this and of Worcester Park adjoining, were felled by those destructive and avaricious rebels in the late war which defaced one of the stateliest seats His Majesty had.

The execution of Charles I on 30 January 1649 marked the end of the use of Nonsuch as a royal palace, although following the Restoration in 1660 the Palace and both parks

23 Nonsuch Palace excavations and Cherry Orchard Farm, 1959.

24 Tudor pottery from the Nonsuch Palace excavations.

25 Flint and chalk wall by Nonsuch Mansion that could date back to the time of the Palace.

were restored to Henrietta Maria. After her death, the palace and parks were granted to trustees on behalf of Barbara, Countess of Castlemaine, a mistress of Charles II, who had been made Baroness of Nonsuch, Countess of Southampton and Duchess of Cleveland. She had the palace demolished and sold off as building materials after the King signed the necessary warrant in 1682. The proceeds helped pay some of Barbara's gambling debts. Although she has often been accused of vandalism, given the cost of maintaining such an elaborate structure, it is difficult to see what else she could have done. Barbara Castlemaine died in 1709. In 1731 the Nonsuch Estate was sold off, the Little Park and the Great Park, by then known as Worcester Park, going to separate purchasers. Worcester Park will be referred to later.

Joseph Thompson bought the Little Park and later, in 1799, ownership passed to Samuel Farmer, who employed the architect Jeffry Wyatt (later Sir Jeffry Wyattville) to design the mansion that was built in 1802-6 and which still graces the park. The kitchen wing of the mansion incorporates part of an earlier house believed to have been made from one of the outbuildings of the Palace.

To return to Ewell, in 1577 there was a survey of the parish for Elizabeth I in which reference was made to the great common field of Southfield and three commons. There were 63 dwellings. The biggest landowner was

26 The Mansion, Nonsuch Park, in 1999. It was built in 1802-6 by the architect Jeffry Wyatt.

27 London Road entrance to Nonsuch Park, *c.*1910. The fountain is a memorial to Charlotte Farmer who died in 1906.

Nicholas Saunder, who held about 340 acres, while Elizabeth Horde of Fitznells came next with 252 acres. At a cross-roads in the centre of the village stood a market house which was pulled down in the latter half of the 18th century; however, some of the other buildings mentioned in the survey still stand.

Ewell in the 17th Century

In 1618 Henry Lloyd, lord of the manor, was granted a licence to hold a market in Ewell. There were complaints around 1620 that the town was poorly served in respect of a parson. 'The Towne is served by a poore old man who is halfe blinde, and by reason of his age can scarcely read.'

There seems not to have been any serious fighting in Ewell in the Civil War although during the Royalist uprising in 1648 there was a skirmish on the outskirts of the town near Nonsuch Palace, followed by a more serious engagement outside Kingston in which about 20 Cavaliers were slain.

The Hearth Tax

Charles II returned in 1660 at the Restoration, and two years later Parliament passed an Act 'for establishing an additional Revenue upon his Majestie, his heires and successors, for the better support of his and their Crown and dignity'. Under the act the occupier of every house in the kingdom had to pay two shillings a year on every chimney hearth, unless exempted by poverty. Industrial hearths were also exempt.

Records of the application of the tax in Ewell in 1664 have survived and provide information on who lived in the parish at that time and in what sort of style. There were 74 chargeable house occupiers who were responsible for 262 hearths. The highest assessment, 13 hearths, was for Timothy Cutler, whose house was in Church Street. Widow Peirce, and several other people, had only one hearth. The Act remained in force until 1689.

28 Jettied houses in the High Street dating from the late 16th century, as seen in 1911.

29 Timber-framed building from the late 16th century at the High Street/Cheam Road junction as seen in 1911. Now part of *The Star* public house.

Chapter Four

Ewell in the 18th Century and the Glyn Family

Ewell in the 18th Century

The replies to the questionnaire for the bishop's visitation of 1725 gave the population of Ewell as 583. There were 50 Presbyterian dissenters, there were no schools, and the patron of the church was the Lord Chancellor.

By the time of the 1788 visitation the population was given as about 500 and the only dissenters were five or six papists. There was one academy not endowed, with about forty scholars and one endowed school with about sixteen scholars. The patron of the church was Sir George Glyn (the second baronet).

In 1730 Ewell manor came into the hands of Lord John Russell, afterwards the Duke of Bedford, who in 1755 sold it to Edward Northey and the Northey family have been lords of the manor ever since, but not resident lords of the manor: they resided in Epsom until 1939. At the time of writing the lord of the manor is Mr. Martin Northey, but the lordship is in the process of being conveyed to Mr. Jack Connolly who is also lord of the manor of East Cheam, West Cheam and Cuddington.

In 1736 Richard Glyn married Susannah Lewen of Ewell who was to inherit a considerable amount of property in the town, and founded the Glyns of Ewell baronetcy that dominated the parish well into the 20th century.

30 Spring House, built in the mid-18th century and clad with mathematical tiles.

31 The mansion built by Philip Rowden, *c*.1770, later known as Garbrand Hall and eventually Bourne Hall, seen here shortly before its demolition in 1962.

32 The 'dog gate' built for Thomas Hercey Barritt, owner of Garbrand Hall, 1796 to 1817, photographed in 1999.

33 The Turrets, built as the dairy of Garbrand Hall, designed by Henry Kitchen, junior, a local man who also designed Ewell Castle. The Turrets was demolished in 1967.

34 One of two Coade stone statues at the end of Bourne Hall Lake seen through the water wheel that is being restored.

The Ewell gunpowder mills went into production in 1754.

A significant event in about 1770 was the building of a mansion on the site of the present Bourne Hall by Philip Rowden, a wealthy London vintner; it was significant because it typified how London merchants were building homes for themselves in Ewell, encouraged by the stage coach service to London (there was a regular service to Epsom as early as 1684).

A workhouse was set up by enlarging the 'pest house' in 1781. The implementation of the Poor Laws involved much harsh treatment of the poor, particularly those not considered to be the responsibility of the parish. Kindness and humanity were not entirely lacking, however and, given the difficult social conditions, it seems likely that the poor of Ewell fared better than in many other parishes. It is significant that, after the workhouse proper was set up in 1781, relief was still being provided for people not living in the workhouse. In some parishes it was a matter of 'Go into the Workhouse or go without'.

The Glyns of Ewell

A visitor to Ewell can hardly fail to notice the name 'Glyn': there is Glyn House, used for educational purposes, and the little Glyn Hall off Cheam Road, as well as Glyn Close, Glyn Road and Glyn School. Until a few years ago the public house near Ewell East Station was called the *Glyn Arms*. In St Mary's Church there are numerous memorial tablets for members of the Glyn family.

The Glyns were important in the affairs of Ewell for more than 200 years, from 1736 when Richard Glyn acquired an interest in the town through marriage to Susannah Lewen, to 1946, when Miss Margaret Glyn died. Richard Glyn was the founder of the Ewell Glyn baronetcy. Surprisingly, during this period of 210 years only four generations were involved; the explanation is that three of the Glyn baronets had second marriages to much younger women and this spread out the generations.

William Lewen

William Lewen, a London merchant, acquired property in Ewell including the rectory in 1709. He was Lord Mayor of London in 1717 and was knighted. As well as the Ewell, Surrey, property he owned farms and estates in other counties. Sir William Lewen died without issue and his property went to three sons of his brother George, one of whom had a daughter Susannah whom Richard Glyn married in 1736. The *Gentleman's Magazine* commented that she was worth £30,000. The Ewell estate together with the manor of Little Hinton, Dorset, a farm at Little Hinton and other properties in Gloucestershire and London were eventually passed onto Richard Glyn.

Richard Glyn, 1711–73, the First Glyn Baronet

Richard Glyn was a prominent drysalter or oilman in Hatton Garden and a man of substance in the city of London. (A drysalter was a dealer in chemicals and dyes such as cochineal, indigo and madder.) At the age of 41 he became a founder partner of a bank which opened in January 1754 as the Vere, Glyn and Hallifax Bank. The wealth from the properties left to Richard Glyn by Robert Lewen in 1751 and from his wife's dowry on their marriage in 1736 would have facilitated the setting up of the bank. Bank records show that many of the early customers were silk merchants and it is unlikely to be a coincidence that the dyes that Richard Glyn dealt with as a drysalter would have been essential in the production of silk goods, which was an important industry in London in the 18th century. Richard's father, Robert, had also been a drysalter.

Richard Glyn had been knighted in 1752 when he was Sheriff of the City. He was Lord Mayor in 1758-9. On 23 September 1759 he was made a baronet. He was a Member of Parliament for the City from 1758 to 1768 and then M.P. for Coventry. He was also Vice-president of the Honourable Artillery Company, a Colonel in the City Militia and

35 Sir Richard Glyn, by Zoffany. The painting is in King Edward's School now at Witley, Surrey. It was originally the Bridewell Royal Hospital of which Sir Richard Glyn was President.

There were three sons by the second wife, Elizabeth Carr, two of whom reached maturity. Richard Carr Glyn inherited the Glyn share of the bank and Thomas Glyn had a distinguished career as a Colonel in the Grenadier Guards. Richard Carr Glyn became a senior partner in the Bank, was knighted in 1791 and became Lord Mayor in 1798, after which he was made a baronet (1st Baronet Glyn of Gaunts). In 1796 he was elected to Parliament for St Ives. From 1798 to 1833 he was President of Bridewell Hospital as his father had been earlier. Elizabeth, the second wife of Richard Glyn, outlived her husband by more than 40 years, dying in 1814.

The bank that Richard Glyn helped to found had various changes of name over the years. In 1969 it was Glyn, Mills and Co. prior to a merger with Williams Deacon's Bank Ltd., whereupon it became Williams and Glyn's Bank, which in 1985 was merged with the Royal Bank of Scotland.

President of the Bridewell and Bethlem Hospitals. A picture emerges of an energetic, competent man who was trusted by his peers and one can see these qualities in the painting of him by Zoffany.

Richard's wife Susannah died in 1751 and in 1754 when he was 43 he married the 17-year-old Elizabeth, daughter of Sir Robert Carr, one of the chief silk merchants of Ludgate Hill. Sir Richard Glyn had three sons by Susannah but only one, George, reached maturity and it was he who inherited the baronetcy and the Ewell property on the sudden death of his father in 1773.

Sir George Glyn, 1739–1814, the Second Baronet

George Glyn was 34 when his father Sir Richard died in 1773 and he became the 2nd baronet. George Glyn married Jane Lewes and they had two sons, Richard, who became a major in the army and died at St Domingo at the age of 26 in 1795 and William who died in infancy. George Glyn's wife Jane died in 1790 and in 1796 at the age of 57 he married the 26-year-old Catherine Powell, by whom he had two sons, Lewen Powell and George Lewen, and a daughter, Anna Margaret.

Sir George, the 2nd baronet, played his part in public life as a Justice of the Peace and a Turnpike Trustee. He was also a Colonel in the 8th Surrey Regiment of Militia.

Chapter Five

Crime and Punishment in Ewell

In early medieval times the manorial courts dispensed justice, but by the 14th century, with the appointment of Justices of the Peace by the Crown, the manorial courts were able to deal with only trivial matters. Otherwise, offenders would be brought before a Justice, who would, in the case of minor offences, deal with the matter himself, or refer it to the Petty Sessions or the Quarter Sessions. The Quarter Sessions had jurisdiction over most indictable offences, but it was left to the discretion of the justices to refer the more difficult cases to the Assizes. Although, in the 15th and 16th centuries, death sentences were frequently pronounced at

Quarter Sessions, later it became the practice to send all capital cases to the Assizes. Since the death sentence could be passed on a felon who had stolen only a few shillings, the Assizes would have been overloaded had not the lower courts found ways of manipulating the nominal value of stolen goods.

Ewell came within Epsom Petty Sessions Division which included parishes that were in the old administrative areas, the Hundreds, of Copthorne and Effingham. The magistrates met at irregular intervals although there was usually at least one meeting every month. Records for the period 1784-93 show that most of the

36   The Watch House in Church Street in an 1825 watercolour.

27

meetings were at the Albion Coffee House in Epsom, although the *Spread Eagle*, also in Epsom, is occasionally mentioned. Four or five magistrates were normally present at each meeting. Sir George Glyn (the 2nd baronet) was frequently listed, and his fellows included William Northey, the Rev. J. Whately of Nonsuch Park, and Joseph Shaw, who owned numerous properties in Epsom and Ewell.

The Quarter Sessions met at various Surrey towns, with an occasional meeting at Epsom. In recent times Guildford and Kingston were the main venues.

The early Assizes were held in Guildford, the county town, but later other towns were involved and eventually Kingston-upon-Thames became the normal venue. We are fortunate that the Assize records have survived for most of the reigns of Elizabeth and James I and provide much information on the trials that took place in that period.

The Assizes in the reign of Elizabeth I

Ewell people were involved in 24 indictments. Four were for sheep stealing, two for horse stealing, seven for general larceny, five were repeated charges of recusancy against the same people, one for dispossessing someone of his property, two were for witchcraft, one was for murder, one for wounding and one was against a constable who negligently allowed a prisoner to escape.

Five people were sentenced to hang, one to be whipped, one was fined, three were allowed benefit of clergy, one died in prison awaiting trial, four were found not guilty and the recusants were proclaimed according to statute. The sentences in the other cases are unclear. Typical examples of these indictments are:

Southwark Assizes, 13 December 1564
Eden Worsley of Ewell, spinster, indicted for murder by witchcraft. On 4 July 1564 at Ewell she bewitched to death Elizabeth Bybye, daughter of Robert Bybye. Tried at the next Assizes and found guilty: to hang.

Croydon Assizes, 28 February 1569
Thomas Tyckner of Ewell, labourer, indicted for grand larceny. On 23 September 1568 he broke into the close of William Saunders Esq. and stole a grey horse (26s. 8d.). Guilty: to hang.

Southwark Assizes, 14 February 1588
John Ricatts, constable of Ewell, indicted for a voluntary escape. On 2 November 1587 Ricatts arrested Alan Cox, innholder, by virtue of a warrant issued by Richard Burton, J.P., but on the same day voluntarily allowed him to escape. Confessed to a negligent escape and submitted to his fine.

Croydon Assizes, 3 July 1592
George Goodhelp of Nonsuch, yeoman, indicted for felonious killing. On 6 May 1592 at Ewell he attacked Robert Brice with a dagger, inflicting wounds from which he died on the following day. Guilty: allowed clergy.

(Felons who could read could escape the noose by pleading 'benefit of clergy' and successfully reading a passage from the Bible. A woman might escape by claiming 'benefit of belly' if she was pregnant, whereby she could escape hanging until after the child was born. In fact, the majority of women being reprieved in this way were eventually released.)

The Assizes in the reign of James I

Ewell people were involved in 12 indictments. Six were for grand larceny, including horse and cattle stealing, three for petty larceny, one for murder and two for recusancy. Four were sentenced to hang, six to be whipped and the recusants were proclaimed and fined.

Typical examples of these indictments are as follows:

Kingston Assizes, 9 July 1607
Charles Godden of Ewell, labourer, indicted for grand larceny. On 1 May 1607 at Ewell he stole a pair of garters (2d.), a silver-gilt ring (3s.), two pairs of hose (2s.) and 1s. in money from John Waterer. Guilty—allowed clergy but unable to read: to hang.

Southwark Assizes, 3 March 1614
Joan Gregorie of Ewell, spinster, indicted for grand larceny. On 27 September 1613 at Ewell she stole a kirtle (4s.), a hat (4s.), a pair of stockings (2s.), a cupboard cloth (1s.) and several pieces of linen (£1) from John Pancke. Guilty to the value of 10d.: whipped.

Croydon Assizes, 27 June 1621
John Rowse of Ewell, miller, indicted for murder. On 21 March 1621 he took Elizabeth and Mary, his daughters, from their beds and drowned them in a little running brook. Confessed: to hang.

Public Executions

It was in the period from the 16th to the 18th centuries that the public execution developed into something akin to a theatrical performance, at which the leading actor was expected to make a gallows speech, expressing contrition. That so many criminals in this predicament did speak of their remorse rather than hurling abuse at the spectators can only be explained by the hold of religion and the efforts made by the prison chaplain to convince the condemned that such confessions were good for the soul. Also, there would have been a desire to conform to the stereotype that had been established.

Although the gallows speech seems to us macabre, in fact it may have helped the poor wretch on the scaffold by taking his mind off the finale of the performance in which he would no longer have a speaking part.

Executions were a source of income to the keepers of gaols: they charged for viewing the condemned prisoner in the death cell. In a pathetic letter to her mother from the Guildford death cell, a woman to be hanged for breaking and entering asked for her best clothes to be sent to her, 'for I have a great many visitors each day.'

According to Manning and Bray, it was once customary for the executioner to demand, and by some means to obtain, 6s. 8d. from the criminal on his (or her) way to execution. This inhuman practice was discontinued on 16 July 1799.

Chapter Six

The Changes taking Place

Before the beginning of the 19th century, Ewell could be regarded as a rural backwater, but changes were about to come. The enclosure of the parish in 1802-3 made agriculture more efficient and more farms were set up. Education became more accessible with the opening of the National School in 1815. Then came the railways, with a station at East Ewell in 1847 and one at West Ewell in 1859. The West Ewell station did much to speed up the development of the area we now know as West Ewell. Study of census returns is a useful indicator of the changes taking place.

With regard to the links with Cuddington, it is of interest that in 1805 all Surrey parishes were assessed for the penalties incurred by the county for not having provided the number of militia men that it should. The assessment was on a proportional basis and the figure for Cuddington was 6s. 8d. against £26 for Ewell. It is clear that for administrative purposes, such as census returns, Cuddington was lumped with Ewell. When the Epsom Poor Law Union was constituted in 1836, Cuddington was one of the 15 parishes that it comprised.

The joint meetings of the manorial courts were still taking place. At a typical meeting on 22 October 1840 the Ewell/Cuddington Court appointed jurors, constables, aleconners and a bailiff, although it is likely that by then these functions would have been largely ceremonial. The manorial system was effectively ended in 1922 by an Act of Parliament that abolished copyholds and converted such tenancies into freeholds. However, the title of lord of Cuddington Manor remains: it was held by the Northey family until 1993, when it was conveyed to Mr. Jack Connolly of Cheam.

The New Poor Law of 1834 brought changes to the treatment of the poor. A large Union Workhouse was built in Epsom and this took in the poor previously housed in the Ewell Workhouse in West Street.

Although a full census in England and Wales was made in 1801, it was not until the 1841 census that detailed returns were made that can be analysed to throw light on how people lived and what they worked at. A study made of the six census returns from 1841 to 1891 shows the variations in the pattern of work over that period. In spite of a total population increase from 1,560 to 2,570, the number of male agricultural workers dropped from 168 to 98. There were still plenty of farms in Ewell in 1891, but the introduction of machinery and more efficient farming methods were having an effect.

The building of big houses in the parish, particularly after the coming of the railways, had an impact on employment and the economy. The 15 male gardeners of 1841 had

risen to 51 in 1891 and domestic servants from 25 to 62. Women domestics went up from 104 to 249. In the managerial, professional and clerical men category the increase was from 14 to 64. Ewell Castle, built for Thomas Calverley by Henry Kitchen in 1811, was employing 10 live-in servants in 1841.

During the Victorian years there were very few wives who worked for a wage—they would have been kept fully occupied with their household chores and looking after the family. In common with the rest of the country in the 19th century, many Ewell wives had large families—it was commonplace to find as many as eight children listed on the census form and in some cases the actual figure would have been higher if one took into account the children who had grown old enough to move away from home. Not only humble families had a large number of children; some of the more affluent ones did also. Captain and Mrs. Harriet Lempriere living in the so-called Manor House in Cheam Road had eight children by 1841. It was said locally that the Lemprieres built an extra room onto the house for every new arrival. In 1891 Edith, the wife of Reginald Jacomb, a wool broker, living at Ewell House,

37 Ewell Castle, built for Thomas Calverley by Henry Kitchen in 1811, seen in a lithograph by G.F. Prosser in 1822.

38 In 1846 Euphemia (Effie) Gray was invited to a dance at Ewell Castle and met John Everett Millais. The couple married in 1855, after Effie's disastrous marriage to John Ruskin in 1848 had been annulled.

39 A.W. Gadesden, seen outside the door of Ewell Castle.

had eight children. She had nine servants to make life tolerable for her.

The number of children under 12 years of age rose over the 50 years from 400 to 749; nevertheless, the proportion of children to the total population remained fairly steady at around 29 per cent.

The most common age for poorer children to start work was 12 years. Most went into unskilled manual work or into domestic service. Some boys were apprenticed to craftsmen, shopkeepers or tradesmen. Sons from more wealthy families followed their fathers into business or took qualifications in other professions: the daughters often stayed at home and took up such pastimes as painting, needlework and music.

Craftsmen included blacksmiths, whitesmiths, boot and shoe makers, coopers, tailors, watchmakers, saddlers, collar dressers and wheelwrights. From 1861 to 1881 blacksmith William Shrubb and his wife Mary lived in Kingston Road. In 1871 he was employing two men and a boy. Mary was still there as a widow running the forge in 1891. The forge in question is thought to be that near the *Eight Bells* at which Mr. Gordon Ralph and his son now work. Craftswomen included dressmakers, milliners, needlewomen and shoe binders.

There were slightly more women than men who lived on their investments or rents from property. In most cases they were the widows of wealthy men. The total number of people of independent means was at its highest at 49 in 1841.

Significant dates in the history of 19th-century Ewell are:

1803	The enclosure of the parish
1815	Ewell National School founded following the Education Act of 1811
1831	George Glyn became vicar
1838	Workhouse closed when new Union Workhouse built in Epsom
1840	Rev. George Glyn becomes 4th baronet
1847	Opening of station on London, Brighton and South Coast Railway
1848	Opening of new parish church
1859	Opening of station on London & South Western Railway
1861	National School transferred to West Street
1875	Gunpowder mills closed
1885	Death of Sir George Glyn
1894	Local government functions of Vestry taken over by Parish Council

The population in 1801 was 1,112 and by 1891 this had risen to 2,570.

In spite of the changes throughout the 19th century, Ewell remained a small town overshadowed by nearby Epsom which had overtaken it in size and importance on account of the spa and the races. As well as the dominant Glyn family there were numerous other well-to-do families now living in the area. However, even by the end of the century it was still largely rural, with some 20 farms.

40 & 41 St Mary's Church Hall seen in these architect's sketches was built at the expense of vicar John Thornton in 1894/5. The intention was to provide a small hall for gymnastic classes among the boys of the neighbourhood, besides its use as a centre for parochial work.

Chapter Seven

The Enclosure of Ewell and the Farms

The open field, strip system of cultivation that had been practised since Saxon times was extremely inefficient and a waste of time and labour because each man's strips were widely scattered. The use of common land was not conducive to rearing good cattle, since it provided no shelter and the mingling of cattle led to the spread of diseases among the herds. Landowners began to see the advantages of re-organising the ownership and holding of land so that the strip system could be replaced by large homogeneous farms. This meant a general re-distribution of land, the dispossession of many small landholders and the enclosure of commons.

Enclosures started at least as early as the 16th century and often took the form of arable land and common land being enclosed for sheep at times when there was a great demand for wool. There was, however, a great increase in enclosures towards the end of the 18th century, reaching a peak between 1801 and 1810, driven by the need to produce more crops during the Napoleonic Wars. The Act of Parliament for enclosing Ewell was put forward in 1801 and the awards were made in 1803. The main promoters of the Bill were the Lord of the Manor, William Northey, the rector, Sir George Glyn, the 2nd Baronet who died in 1814, and Thomas Calverley, who owned the three sub-manors as well as other property.

A detailed plan of Ewell was drawn up for the Commissioners in 1802 showing the existing properties and the proposed allotments. It made reference to about 180 houses and cottages in the parish. The plan was drawn to a scale of approximately 18 inches to a mile, and is the earliest large scale map of Ewell in existence. The Commissioners were expected to defray their expenses by selling off bits of common land and some 130 acres of common land were lost by this, from Ewell Marsh and Ewell Downs. Thomas Calverley bought 111 acres of Ewell Downs for £1,775. Some allotments were made to compensate individuals for loss of rights. William Northey, Lord of the Manor, was given 21 acres of Kingston Common, near Ruxley, in lieu of his manorial right to the soil. Sir George Glyn received nearly 300 acres in lieu of tithes, which included 188 acres of Ewell Common Field. Some 70 landholders, freehold or copyhold, are listed in the schedule and, apart from a few with very small holdings, all received allotments, mostly on the commons, but some on the common field, proportional to their original holdings. Thomas Calverley was allotted nearly 350 acres excluding the land he purchased from the Commissioners, while some allotments were less than half an acre. The Poor of Ewell were allotted just under one acre next to the workhouse, bringing their total holding up to about nine acres.

The Farms

There had been some modification of the early system of strip cultivation prior to the enclosure of Ewell. By purchase and exchange, landholders had built up large units of land that were easier to work. There were in fact at least eight units of land that could be referred to as farms before 1803. The parcelling out of the common land enabled more farms to be set up after that date.

Farming in Ewell reached its peak around 1900 when there were nearly 20 farms. The number went down rapidly after the First World War: there was a great demand for houses and it became profitable to sell off farms for building.

The map on page 36 shows the position of the farmhouses, numbered as follows:

1.	Longdown	11.	Fitznells
2.	The Downs	12.	Warren
3.	North Looe	13.	Cherry Orchard
4.	Priest Hill	14.	Marsh
5.	The Workhouse	15.	Bowling Green
6.	Nonsuch Court	16.	Poplar
7.	West Street	17.	Ewell Court
8.	Cuddington Court	18.	Ruxley
9.	Rectory	19.	Coldharbour
10.	Ewell Castle	20.	Worcester Park

Although we are mainly concerned with the old parish of Ewell, a few farms that were not in the parish but were within the present boundaries of Ewell have been included. A detailed description of all the farms is beyond the scope of this book but the following will be mentioned:

Longdown Farm

Longdown Farm was carved out of the common land that was allotted to Thomas Calverley in the Enclosure Awards of 1803. He also owned Fitznells, North Looe and Ruxley farms. In fact, after the awards he had a total of nearly 1,000 acres of land in Ewell and was the biggest landowner.

The Longdown farmland was at the southern end of the parish to the west of Reigate Road. Longdown House, around which the farm was based, was built not long after 1803 and it still stands in Longdown Lane, as do two of the barns. An entry in the Vestry minutes of 1827 suggests that the main crop at that time was wheat.

North Looe Farm

North Looe Farm was in existence in 1803 at the time of the Enclosure Awards, in which it was described as a freehold farmhouse and homestead, with 114 acres. The owner was Thomas Calverley. The land was towards the southern end of the parish to the east of the Reigate Road. In 1837 North Looe Farm was run in conjunction with Fitznell's Farm and it would appear administered from the latter.

As a result of the Small Holdings and Allotments Act of 1908, Surrey County Council bought North Looe Farm in 1910 and leased much of it to the Epsom Small Holdings Society. They also had some twenty cottages built for the smallholders.

Much of the North Looe area is still open ground and some of the smallholdings have been reunited in recent years to form Beeches Farm, which has about ninety acres and is the only working farm left in Ewell.

Priest Hill Farm

Priest Hill Farm was made on the Southfield out of land awarded to Sir George Glyn (the 2nd baronet) in lieu of tithes. Rectory Farm was also owned by Sir George Glyn and the two farms were run in conjunction with each other. It seems that both were run from Rectory Farm.

By 1899 Priest Hill Farm was owned by Edward Martin of Nonsuch Court Farm and his bailiff occupied the farmhouse. The farm lands stretched across the Banstead Road. Priest Hill Farm had direct access to what is now Ewell East Station, where there was a siding for unloading truck loads of manure which came from London stables. In the 1930s John Wallace was the farmer. He had many acres of potatoes and gypsies came once a year to help pick them up.

After the Second World War, the farm was bought up as the site for the technical college and playing fields and in 1956 the farm buildings were demolished. They stood about 150m east of the college.

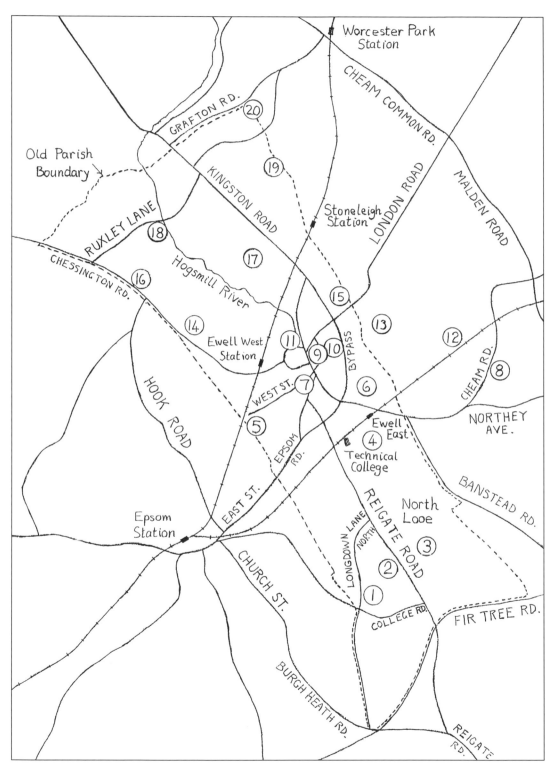

42   The farms of Ewell.

43   A barn in Church Street that belonged to Rectory Farm, photographed in 1994.

Rectory Farm

The Rectory Farm went with the Rectory Estate, which came into the possession of the Glyn family in the 18th century. The farmhouse which was demolished in 1905 had Tudor features. The area of the farm in 1802 was just over 23 acres. Something belonging to the farm that has survived is the barn in Church Street, which is a five-bay building with a roof of queen-post construction.

The census of 1851, the most important year in respect of the Pre-Raphaelite connection with Ewell, shows William Hobman, the uncle of Holman Hunt, living at Rectory Farm. By 1895 the farmhouse was being used as a private residence. When it was demolished the site became part of the grounds of Rectory House and an extension to the churchyard.

Fitznells

Fitznell's Manor is a building that came down in the world, from manor house to farmhouse. It includes an early 17th-century, three-gabled addition to a remnant of an early 16th-century manor house.

In 1803 Fitznells was a farm owned by Thomas Calverley and it appears that sometimes it was worked in conjunction with the Calverley farm at North Looe. That was so in 1841 when the two farms comprised 333 acres.

Thomas Pocock, a local carrier who wrote reminiscences of Ewell in the period 1905 to 1930, refers to the farm as being run by a Mrs. Clara Isobel Curtis with her two sons, William and Charlie. The Curtis's had two dairy shops, one in Ewell High Street and the other in Balham High Road.

44 Phyllis Lavender with a Cherry Orchard Farm milk cart, *c*.1923.

45 C.I. Curtis (Fitznells Farm) milk float, *c*.1923. They had a dairy shop in Ewell High Street.

In 1915 the farm was surveyed with a view to conversion to smallholdings. The report refers to heavy soil, 13 horses, 50 cows, 200 poultry, 2 cottages, 12 men, ample implements and a good style of farming. The acreage of 112 included 50 acres of arable and 50 of grass. The smallholding plan fell through and in 1927-33 the farmland was developed by Modern Homes and Estates Limited.

The farmhouse became a dwelling that housed a music school for some years until 1988 when the building was refurbished as offices. It is now used as doctors' surgeries.

Cherry Orchard Farm

Cherry Orchard Farm was very close to the site of Nonsuch Palace; in fact some of the buildings were inside what was the privy garden and the remainder in the Wilderness and the Orchard.

The census returns for 1841 and 1851 show that the farm was occupied by market gardeners. Pocock says that in the first quarter of the 20th century it was farmed by Joe Lavender as a pig farm and market garden, but they must also have had a few cows according to a 1923 photograph of Phyllis Lavender with a milk cart. The farm as it was in 1959 can be seen in the photograph of the Nonsuch Palace excavations in Chapter Three.

The demolition carried out in the 1970s was thorough and the area is now completely overgrown. Cherry Orchard Farm was bought for the public in 1935 and is administered by Epsom and Ewell Borough Council.

46 Carts belonging to Thomas Pocock, a local carrier, who wrote some interesting reminiscences of Ewell in the first part of the 20th century.

47 Edward Waterer Martin, owner of Nonsuch Court Farm for a long period before the First World War. He was a successful businessman with investments that included shares in the Sutton and District Water Company, of which he was chairman for many years. He was still chairman at the age of 97 when he died in 1933.

Bowling Green Farm

When the Nonsuch Estate was split up in 1731, the Great Park, by then known as Worcester Park, was divided into a number of farms, one of which was Bowling Green Farm. It is assumed to have taken its name from the bowling green of Nonsuch Palace which was immediately to the north of the palace and about 500 yards from the farmhouse. The farmhouse itself stood in Elmwood Drive and showed three main periods of construction ranging from the mid-18th century to the third quarter of the 19th.

In 1841 both Bowling Green and Coldharbour farms were being run jointly: the combined acreage was 141. By 1861 the farms seem to have split, but by 1871 they were together again.

In 1860 the farms had been acquired by John Jeffries Stone. He had a large house he called Stoneleigh built close to the Bowling Green Farmhouse. It gave its name to the Stoneleigh district. Particulars for an auction sale in 1882, after the death of J.J. Stone, described Stoneleigh as a handsome mansion with pleasure grounds, stabling and cottages and a park-like land. The stabling comprised seven loose boxes and a six-stall stable, together with a coach house and harness room, and appeared to have been accommodated within what had been the Bowling Green Farmhouse. Stoneleigh House was long ago demolished but the former farmhouse stood until 1997. It was known as Ewell Park House and was a students' hostel. Presumably the stables had been converted back to living accommodation.

Worcester Park Farm

Worcester Park Farm was the most northerly of the farms we are concerned with. The farmhouse stood close to the junction of The Avenue, Royal Avenue and Delta Road. It was an ancient building that is thought to have been a keeper's lodge (keeper with a small 'k') that stood close to the original Worcester House, which was the residence of the Keeper of the Great Park of Nonsuch (Keeper with a capital 'K') and acquired its name when the Earl of Worcester was the Keeper. In the Parliamentary Survey of the Nonsuch Estate in 1650, the keeper's lodge is described as a sizeable timbered house of two storeys, with seven rooms on the first floor and various out-buildings. It stood in its own grounds with a garden, well planted orchard, a green court and two yards.

When Worcester House was demolished the keeper's lodge was left standing. The farm was probably created towards the end of the 18th century. The 1802 survey shows it as having 85 acres.

Holman Hunt and John Millais stayed at Worcester Park Farm for several months in 1851, working on the backgrounds of some of

48   The Hogsmill River provided the background for Millais' *Ophelia in the Stream*. He worked on the painting when staying at Worcester Park Farm in 1851. Ophelia herself was Elizabeth Siddal, immersed in a bathtub in the studio. In the process she got chilled to the bone and was unwell for months.

49   Park Farm House, *c.*1914. William Hobman, uncle of Holman Hunt, was living there in 1871. It had previously been known as Marsh Farm. The farm came partly out of the 1803 Enclosure Awards.

50 West Street Farm barns shortly before demolition in 1913. West Street Council School was built on the site. In 1803 the farm was owned by the Trustees of William Jubb, who manufactured paper at the Lower Mill.

51 When Ewell Court Farm was demolished in 1931 the great barn was dismantled and re-erected at *Great Fosters Hotel* near Egham. The farm had been originally associated with Ewell Manor, Worth Court.

52 Mr. Gordon Ralph at work in the Ewell forge in 1994. The forge is said to have been there for nearly 300 years, and was essential to local farmers for shoeing horses and making tools.

53 Harvesting near Chessington Road, Ewell, *c.*1890.

the paintings that helped to make them famous. Millais' letters from Worcester Park Farm to his friends, Mr. and Mrs. Coombe, have survived and provide an interesting account of the episode. Millais refers to it as a jolly bachelor party, since, as well as Holman Hunt, his friend Charlie Collins and brother William Millais were there for part of the time. The major paintings that Holman Hunt worked on at Ewell in 1851 were *The Hireling Shepherd* and *The Light of the World*. John Millais worked on *Ophelia in the Stream* and *The Huguenot*. The background of *The Huguenot* was a brick wall at Worcester Park Farm.

Worcester Park Farm did not survive long after 1851. It was demolished prior to the building in 1873 of a mansion, Worcester Court, which in 1940 became a private school. The building was demolished in 1959. The lodge of Worcester Court, also built in 1873, in the same style as the mansion, survives in an enlarged form.

Chapter Eight

Schools

The National Society for Promoting the Education of the Poor in the Principles of the Established Church throughout England and Wales was established in 1811 and the Ewell National School was set up in 1815 in a couple of cottages in Old Schools Lane which were demolished in 1964. The foundation was helped by contributions from local charities, particularly Brumfields and Whites, and later, in 1860, the school received £200 in consequence of the will of Thomas Calverley. When an official inspection was made in 1846, 41 boys were present, of whom 15 were able to read with ease: there were 55 girls, 17 of whom were able to read with ease. The age of admission was 5 years and the age of leaving 13 years. The children each paid one penny per week. From 1854, 20 poor children were nominated yearly by the Vestry to receive free education.

In 1861 a new National School was opened in West Street. It has been described as a fine building according to the standards of the times, and is today a Listed Building. The site where previously three cottages had stood was donated by Sir George Glyn. There was a large lower room for boys, a large upper room for girls and a smaller room for mixed infants divided from the boys' room by a screen. A

54 Ewell National School started in 1815 in a building in Old Schools Lane. When the school was transferred to a new building in West Street in 1861 the old building was converted to cottages and remained in use for many years before it became neglected and was eventually demolished.

55   The 1861 school in West Street photographed in 1992, when it was no longer a school.

56   West Street Boys School, Classroom 4, in 1961.

house for the headmaster stood at the east end of the school and one for the headmistress at the west end.

In 1862 head teachers were instructed to keep daily records in a log book, and the log books written up by the succession of head-masters and headmistresses give fascinating glimpses of school life. Some of the heads were long-serving. Miss Deavin was in charge of the Girls School from 1861 until 1902. Mr. S. Buxton was headmaster of the Boys School from 1882 to 1915.

In National Schools religious instruction was an important part of the curriculum and the Rev. Sir George Glyn and his curates visited frequently to give scripture lessons to each department. There were annual reports on the schools by government inspectors: those from the Infants School were usually favourable. The June 1867 report said, 'The school continues in an excellent state of order. The children are

happy, intelligent and well grounded.' The annual examinations in religious education were always satisfactory in all three departments.

The Inspectors' reports for the Girls School were not always glowing: arithmetic and spelling were frequently stated to be poor, and the needlework was only fair. However, geography was nearly always praised. The Boys' School did well in inspections and examina-tions: successes by Mr. Buxton's pupils in 1896 included a Free Studentship at the School of Art and Wood Carving, South Kensington and two County Council Scholarships.

A reminder that Ewell was a rural area is that the August holiday was known as the harvest holidays and in 1871 it was extended for a week 'as gleaning was not yet over'. Pupils were frequently absent on account of country pursuits that included ploughing matches, sheep minding, acorn picking, haymaking and potato picking.

As might be expected, the epidemics prevalent in the second half of the 19th century are reflected in the log books. The school had to be closed for three weeks in 1874 because of an outbreak of measles in which two boys died. In 1879 scarlet fever caused closure for ten weeks. Diphtheria, mumps, whooping cough and smallpox also figure in the entries.

Not only boys were punished for misdemeanours by caning, as the log book for the Girls School shows. On 15 March 1912 Lydia Lawrence and Emily Whittington were caned for exchanging notes with boys.

In 1916 the Girls and Infants' Department was transferred to a new Council School nearby in West Street. The boys then had the 1861 building to themselves and the school retained its connection with the church. In 1971 the boys were transferred to a new school that was opened on the Longmead Estate. The 1916 building became the Ewell Grove County First School and the 1861 building became its annexe. It was later used for storage by the Surrey Record Office and went out of use in 1999 when the new History Centre was opened in Woking. At the time of writing there is a proposal to turn the 1861 building into flats.

Today, the 1916 building is the Ewell Grove County First Infants School.

The boys' department of the Ewell National School gave rise to the Ewell Old Boys, an association that held its first reunion on 11 April 1909 with a social gathering in Ewell Lecture Hall, presided over by the school headmaster, Mr. Samuel Buxton. The programme consisted mainly of songs and recitations, and terminated with the national anthem: light refreshments and cigars were to be provided in the hall at moderate charges.

57   Ewell Infants Class 3, 1907.

58   Class of boys at Ewell National School, September 1896.

The Ewell Old Boys flourished and their annual reunion became an important event in the local social calendar. A typical programme for a reunion on 20 June 1931 started with sports in the Rectory Grounds by permission of Sir Arthur Glyn, who was President of the Old Boys as well as the honorary treasurer. The sports were followed by Sir Arthur placing a wreath on the Ewell Roll of Honour. At 5.15 p.m. came tea and a social gathering in the Rectory grounds and later a concert in the Music Room succeeded by dancing on the lawns.

It is clear that the old Boys kept in touch with members who had left Ewell, since as well as a general secretary, they had secretaries for provincial and overseas members. The organisation owed much to the sponsorship of Sir Arthur Glyn, and did not survive for long after his death in 1942.

Private Schools

There have been numerous private schools in Ewell, but these are outside the scope of the present study and only brief references will be made to a few of the more outstanding ones.

William Monger started Monger's Academy, Epsom Road, in 1809. In 1851 it had 54 boarders. It shut down in about 1859 and the building is now used as an Abbeyfield Home for elderly people.

The Grange School, Kingston Road, had 15 girl boarders in 1851. In 1871 it is shown as having 82 boarding boys, many of whom had parents working in India.

Parkside School, Kingston Road, was founded in 1879. By the 1920s there was accommodation for 45 boarders. It moved from Ewell in 1933 when its grounds were used for housing development. It had a particularly good

59 Class of girls at Ewell National School in the early
20th century.

60 Mr. Reuben Jeal, photographic agent and picture
frame maker, *c.*1900. In about 1895 he became
caretaker of the National School and remained so until
his death in 1921.

61 Procession of Ewell Old Boys in 1917.

62 Ewell Brass Band in 1893, all old boys of Ewell National School except for bandmaster. Second from right in back row is Jesse Beams, son of the postman, and in middle row on extreme right is his brother Alfred.

63   Ewell Adult School outside Mary Wallis Hall in 1923.

reputation, many of its boys going on to some of the top public schools, and it produced an exceptional number of war heroes, including three holders of the Victoria Cross.

Ewell Castle, Church Street, the largest house in Ewell, became a boys school in 1926. Today, the sixth form is co-educational and there is an associated co-educational Junior School in nearby Spring Street.

Bourne Hall, the forerunner of the present community centre, was a school 'for the daughters of gentlemen' from 1931 until 1953.

The Ewell Adult School

The Ewell Adult School was founded in 1911 as part of a national organisation started by Quakers in 1798. The original aim was to provide basic education for people who had not been to school. The Schools also promoted Christian ethics and good fellowship, so that when free schooling became available to all the Adult Schools still had a role to play, although the educational aspect turned from reading and writing towards extending people's mental horizons by the study of literature and other aspects of life not given overmuch attention in the early free schools.

The Adult School movement reached its peak around 1900, when there were more than 30 schools in Surrey, and a national membership of something like 130,000. Today, it would seem that many people rely on television for their extra-mural education, and the national membership is down to about 1,500. In the face of that decline, it is notable that the Ewell Adult School is still carrying on the tradition of promoting Friendship, Understanding and Knowledge. When first founded it met in the little hall in West Street that had been built for Mary Wallis, a remarkable domestic servant who founded a chapel. Later, the Adult School met in members' homes, and from 1948 in Glyn Hall, then known as the Parochial Room, where it still holds its weekly meetings. Glyn Hall had been left by Miss Margaret Glyn to be used for educational or other similar purposes for the benefit of the inhabitants of Ewell.

Chapter Nine

West Ewell and the Rebirth of Cuddington

West Ewell

West Ewell was known as the Upper and Lower Marsh in the census returns before 1891 when names of roads begin to appear. It is probable that this part of Ewell was subject to flooding, being close not only to the River Hogsmill but also to three of its tributaries— The Bonesgate Stream, The Horton Stream and the Green Lanes Stream. At the 1803 Enclosure Awards, when Chessington Road was known as Marsh Lane, there was just a scattering of cottages over the area, mostly lived in by agricultural labourers and gunpowder workers.

Marsh Farm and Poplar Farm, parts of the farmhouses of which still stand in Heatherside Road and Chessington Road, came out of the Enclosure Awards and by 1841 there was also *The Three Fishes* beer house.

The 1841 Census shows James Baker, a 35-year-old gunpowder maker, living with his family, which included a son James, in a cottage on the Marsh. In 1863 James Junior was to die in an enormous explosion at the gunpowder works, together with Henry Hockham, aged 60 who had also lived on the Marsh since at least 1841, and a Mr. Weaverman. James Baker left a widow, Ann, aged 30 and five children aged between 3 and 11 years.

From 1841 to 1881 there were between 28 and 36 households living in what is now West Ewell, almost all of them labourers and gunpowder workers. By 1891, however, the

64 After 1881 some substantial houses were built in Chessington Road, West Ewell. Photographed in 1999.

65   Chessington Road, West Ewell, *c.*1930.

66   Chessington Road, West Ewell, 1999.

situation had changed dramatically. Nearby West Ewell Station encouraged middle-class commuters to move into the area. There were now 71 households, of which at least twelve were headed by professional or managerial men. They included accounting, banking and clerical staff, woollen trade managers, a retired doctor, a retired engineer, a teacher and a journalist. Most lived in houses newly erected in Chessington Road. Considerable construction work had now taken place including the erection of terraced cottages called Downsview Cottages and Rosebery Cottages. Three larger houses had been built in Fulford Road—Belle Vue, Daisy Villa and Park Villa.

The first mention of shops in West Ewell comes in the 1891 Census with Ann Godfrey, 59, shopkeeper and Joseph Wise, 59, dairyman. By 1895 the *Kelly's Directory* includes John Baker, Chessington Road, general dealer. By 1915 there were a number of shops and service providers. King's Walk, Chessington Road,

houses several—Annie Beams, draper and sub-postmistress, Harry Beams and Richard Webb, butcher. Ten years later Strikes Cash Stores was offering its customers grocery, provisions, hardware, vegetables and fruit.

Spiritual needs began to be catered for in 1865 when a licence was obtained by the Rev. George Glyn, Vicar of St Mary's, Ewell, to erect a building as a school/chapel in 'Ewell Hamlet' in Chessington Road, nearly opposite Plough Road. In 1871 Thomas Parson, 35, was schoolmaster and scripture reader. On a 1913 map the building is still described as a Sunday School. It is now the venue for the West Ewell Social Club.

All Saints Church was built in 1893 in Fulford Road as a daughter church of St Mary's, Ewell. John Henry Bridges of Ewell Court, a descendant of the gunpowder manufacturers, established a fund and donated the plot of land for its construction. West Ewell became an independent parish in 1952.

67 Old cottages in Plough Road, West Ewell, known as the Black Cottages, *c.*1900.

68 The building that was erected as a school/chapel in 'Ewell Hamlet' in 1865, photographed in 1999.

69 All Saints Church, West Ewell, 1999. It was built in 1893 after John Henry Bridges of Ewell Court established a fund and gave a plot of land.

In the 20th century the pattern of change in West Ewell followed the general trend in Ewell—more people moved into the area necessitating the construction of many more houses, schools were provided and shopping facilities were improved. Some older housing still remains. Today West Ewell is still a recognisably separate area but has moved a long way from the agricultural marshy area of the earlier centuries.

70   John Tims in his motor car in 1903. He had lived at Cleeve Cottage in Chessington Road since 1885 and made a name for himself as a photographer of local life over four decades. He died at the age of 83 in 1944.

71   The living room of Cleeve Cottage as photographed by John Tims.

The Rebirth of Cuddington and its Partition

In 1750 Worcester Park had been sold to William Taylor, who had made a fortune from the gunpowder mills that he had built along the Hogsmill River at Malden in 1720. Worcester House, the mansion of the Earl of Worcester, Keeper of the Great Park, was demolished. It had been a four-storey brick building on the high ground at the junction of Royal Avenue and Delta Road. William Taylor junior had a new mansion, Worcester Park House, built in 1799 on a new site to the south-west at the bottom of the hill near the present *Hogsmill Tavern*. It was pulled down shortly after the Second World War.

Much of Worcester Park was divided into farms, which included Bowling Green Farm, Sparrow Farm, Coldharbour Farm and Worcester Park Farm. In 1859 the London

and South Western Railway was extended from Raynes Park to Epsom, including a station now known as Worcester Park. In 1865 the area around Worcester Park Farm was bought by the Landed Estates Company, together with other areas outside the old park boundary, and the development of the modern Worcester Park began. Large houses were built along The Avenue. On the triangular piece of land between The Avenue and St Mary's Road the company had a small corrugated iron church built in 1866 to serve the new estate. The church was known locally as the Iron Church, or sometimes the Tin Church.

Until the development of the Worcester Park area, the population of Cuddington parish was small and consisted of Nonsuch court officials and palace workers plus farmers and farm workers. Later, there were the people associated with the Mansion. Further evidence

72 Following the acquisition of land around Worcester Park Farm in 1865 by the Landed Estates Company, large houses were built along The Avenue, seen here in 1999.

73 St Mary's Church, Cuddington, in 1999. The church was built in 1895 to replace an iron church.

that pre-development Cuddington was a sparsely populated area is provided by the 1861 census returns which give a population of 148 whereas that of Ewell was 1,922. By 1871 the population was up to 375 and this had risen to 774 by 1901, by which time the figure for Ewell was 3,338. The congregation of the Iron Church soon aspired to having a more substantial church erected. By the early 1890s, deterioration of the building made its replacement a matter of urgency. The land on which it stood was acquired so that it could be transferred to the Ecclesiastical Commissioners and with the help of wealthy supporters a new church was built which was consecrated in 1895. It was designed by A. Thomas and built of flint, with a polygonal apse and a fleche. In 1959 the west end of the church was extended with a gallery, choir vestry and new west window by the celebrated glass artist Lawrence Lee. He also designed windows for the rebuilt Coventry Cathedral. There were further improvements in 1994 when the old church hall was demolished and work began on new meeting rooms attached to the west end of the church, which were opened in 1995.

The Ecclesiastical Commissioners considered in 1895 that there was a good opportunity to revive the parish of Cuddington, and the newly built church was declared to be 'the parish church of the parish of Cuddington, in lieu of the old parish church of St Mary (demolished in 1538), as fully in all respects as if the new church of St Mary had been originally the parish church of the same parish.'

The development of the northern end of the old parish was followed by the growth of housing estates in other parts during the 20th century. New populations springing up had made it necessary to create new parishes out of old ones, and adjust boundaries. Part of the parish was lost by the creation of the parish of St Paul, Nork, in 1931 although at that time a portion of the parish of Ewell was annexed to Cuddington. There were further losses in 1948 when St Francis of Assisi, Ruxley Lane and St John the Baptist, Stoneleigh, became independent parishes. They had been daughter churches of St Mary's, Ewell, and had been opened in 1934 and 1935 respectively. Also, in 1948, portions of Cuddington were annexed to the parishes of Ewell, Cheam and St Philip, Cheam Common. The present ecclesiastical parish of Cuddington is the comparatively small area with boundaries that include Worcester Park Road, Highdown, Stoneleigh Avenue, part of Cunliffe Road, Mavis Avenue and Kingston Road. Within this area are the Epsom and Ewell Borough Council ward of Cuddington and part of the ward of Auriol.

As referred to in Chapter Three, Nonsuch Mansion was built in the park by Samuel Farmer. Several generations of the Farmer family lived at the Mansion, the last being Alice Farmer who had married Colonel Francis Colborne. Mrs. Alice Colborne died a widow in 1936, and in 1937 a consortium of local authorities (London and Surrey County Councils and Sutton and Cheam and Epsom and Ewell Corporations) purchased most of the Little Park, and the Mansion. Cherry Orchard Farm that had been in the park had already been bought by Epsom and Ewell Council.

What might have been

Suppose that Henry VIII had not come across Cuddington village when out hunting and it had not become the site of Nonsuch Palace. It is likely that the church would still be there, and that, given its proximity to London, the village would have attracted well-to-do merchants in the same way that Ewell did, so that there could well be some fine 18th- and 19th-century houses. Although Cuddington lacked the gushing springs of water that Ewell had, it is on the spring line and a water supply would not have been a problem. However, without the palace and the park it is unlikely that Cuddington would have escaped being built on: there would be bricks, mortar and concrete all the way from Ewell.

Chapter Ten

Shops and Public Houses

Shops

As a one time market town, Ewell had a few shops at an early date. The market house had stood at the junction of Church Street and High Street: High Street and Green Man Street, the road to Epsom, later to become part of High Street, was the main shopping area. The census returns indicate 16 shops in 1841 and 27 in 1891. The wide range of shops and tradesmen gives the impression that Ewell was largely self-sufficient for its basic commodities. At the later date there were four butchers, five bakers, five grocers, two drapers, a greengrocer, chemist, bootmakers and all the other essential services. Some of the early shops operated from the front rooms of cottages, and even in 1900 there were still some ordinary cottages to be seen in Green Man Street, but more shops came into operation until not a single ground floor dwelling was left. Sadly, Ewell Village has lost many of its down-to-earth shops: they have been replaced by restaurants, estate agents, hairdressers and other less practical establishments.

The old Public Houses

Ewell has had a variety of beerhouses, taverns and inns. A study made by the Documentary Group of Nonsuch Antiquarian Society found references to 18 pubs (to use a modern elastic term) of historic interest, some of which are still with us, while others have been demolished or rebuilt. Many of these pubs became established in the 19th century and so it is convenient to include pubs in Part 2 of this book although some date from before 1800. As well as entries in public records such as court rolls, rate books and census returns, there have been occasional mentions of Ewell pubs in literature. John Taylor, the Water Poet, refers to two taverns in Ewell and Samuel Pepys used

74 The back of a 16th-century timber-framed building in Cheam Road (Nos. 5 and 5a) *c*.1913, when it was occupied by Radford and Clark, Grocers. At one time the yard behind the building contained five cottages and was known as Marfleet's Yard and later Nuthall's Yard. In 1927 Radford and Clark were replaced by P. Nuthall and Co., tea and coffee specialists. The building was demolished in 1968.

75   Parker's Stores in the High Street, 1924.

76   Earle's Stores in the High Street shortly after the Second World War.

JOHN DEAMERY,

FANCY

Bread and Biscuit Baker,

Pastrycook & Confectioner,

HIGH STREET, EWELL.

Families waited on Daily with Pure Home-
Made Bread.

J. B. HARDS,

Family Grocer, Tea=Dealer,

CHEESEMONGER & OILMAN,

HIGH STREET, EWELL.

Begs respectfully to call the attention of Families furnish-
ing, to his superior Stock of China, Glass, Earthenware,
House Brooms, Brushes and Mops, Hair, Hat, Shoe and
Butler's Brushes, House Pails, Door Mats, Woodware,
Wash Leathers, Bowls, with or without handles, Rope and
Twine, Blacking, Black Lead, Heath and Stable Brooms,
Paste and Plate Powders, Housemaid's and Plate Cleaning
Gloves, &c., &c.

WAX, SPERM & COMPOSITE CANDLES.

Huntley & Palmer's Reading Biscuits fresh every week.

China & Glass Repaired & Rivetted on the most approved
principle.

77   *Above left* An advertisement published in 1860.

78   *Above right.* An advertisement published in 1860.

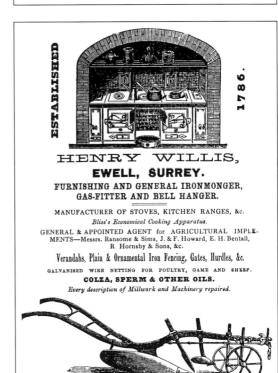

79   *Right.* An advertisement published in 1860. Henry
Willis had his premises at what is now No. 9 High
Street, Ewell.

an inn in Ewell when visiting Nonsuch Palace or Epsom Spa. He became so attached to 'My Besse', a well favoured country lass who served there, that he persuaded her to join his household as a servant.

Brief details of the 18 pubs are as follows:

The Queen's Head, High Street, occupied what is now No. 9 High Street. It is the earliest known hostelry in Ewell and is mentioned, by its earlier name of *The Red Lion*, in Thomas Taylor's Survey of 1577. It was later known as *The Queen Anne*, becoming *The Queen's Head* by about 1760.

The Bull's Head, High Street, stood at the junction of Cheam Road with High Street, where the Midland Bank now is. It is thought to have been built in the 17th century to cater for people travelling to Epsom to take the waters. In the 19th century it was a stopping place for the London coaches, which left at seven and eight o'clock in the morning and at three in the afternoon. It was often the meeting place for the manorial court and the parish vestry and in 1818 the Excise office was situated there. *The Bull's Head* was pulled down in the 1860s.

The King William IV, High Street. The present building, with its elaborate tiled pilasters, dates from the early 19th century, but a public

house has existed on the site for many years before that. In the 17th century it was known as *The George* and by 1828 as *The George and Dragon*, changing its name to *The King William IV* soon after the accession of that monarch.

Archaeological excavations behind the building in 1967-7 revealed a vast amount of Roman material. In 1996 an extension was built at the rear and the name was changed to 'The Friend and Firkin'.

The Hop Pole, West Street, was built in the early 18th century of soft red brick of varying colour, with a brick inter-storey band of three courses projecting a little. Part of the property is known to have been occupied in the early 19th century by Bliss and Willis, who started their blacksmith and ironworking business there before moving to High Street. By 1841 it was known as *The Hop Pole* beerhouse, and was occupied by William Hale, a brewer. From 1850 to 1873 the licensee was Henry Taylor. There is no record of a new landlord succeeding Henry Taylor, and on his departure the property became two cottages, which continued to be known as Hop Pole Cottages. They were demolished in 1973.

The Green Man, High Street. The present *Green Man* was built in the 1930s but there

80 *The Hop Pole* (Hop Pole Cottages), demolished in 1973, in a drawing by Olive Temple.

81   *The Green Man, c.1930.* Behind the pub was the Old Fair Field.

was an inn of that name long before that, standing in what is now the car park. The part of the High Street from Cheam Road to the Reigate Road was once known as Green Man Street. In the days of Ewell Fair, held annually in May and October, the sheep were penned in the Fair Field meadow behind *The Green Man* and the horses were gathered under the garden wall opposite. The 'Pleasure Fair' was held in *The Green Man* yard. The last fair was held in 1890. The earliest mention of *The Green Man* is in the Parish Overseer's accounts for 1763 and it is one of the public houses mentioned in the Vestry minutes from 1763 to 1834 as a place of adjournment at the end of official business.

The Spring Hotel, London Road, dates from the early 19th century and is thought to have become an inn *c.*1820. Cloudesley Willis, a local historian writing around 1930, recalled

that Derby Week was the great event of the year when the landlord could count on taking enough money to pay his year's rent.

The Eight Bells, Kingston Road. The present building dates from about 1905 and is set at the rear of a courtyard flanked by 18th-century cottages. The building on the south side has the unusual feature of a semi-circular front and may once have been a toll cottage. In 1787 the property was described as 'a messuage with brewhouse, garden and stables etc. known as *The Eight Bells*, formerly two tenements occupied by John Griffin, victualler.'

The King's Head, Church Street. Near the entrance to Glyn House stands 'The Cottage', No. 9 Church Street which, with No. 11 adjoining, once constituted *The King's Head Inn*. The present building dates partly from the 19th century but incorporates earlier work including part of a flint cellar possibly of about 1600.

82 *The Spring Hotel* was a popular rendezvous for cyclists in the first half of the 20th century.

J. Edwards in his *Companion from London to Brightelmstone* in 1790 describes the *King's Head* as a 'good public house kept by Mr. Robert Buckland. This is the house of call for the Guildford coach, likewise for road waggons, several of which put up here.'

The coaching trade must have suffered from the opening in 1807 of a new route to Brighton, which did not come through Ewell. A further blow was the building of the new road into the village which avoided Church Street and diverted some of the traffic past what is now *The Spring Hotel*.

In 1838 the Rev. George Glyn had a splendid new mansion built on the site of the old Rectory House, and he must have looked askance at the public house which flanked his main entrance. So in 1850 he bought the pub and had it converted into two dwellings.

The Plough Inn, Plough Road, off Chessington Road, was built between the wars. It replaced an older building which was of early 19th-century date and had a mathematical tiled façade on a timber-framed building. The first name of the beerhouse, which can be traced back to 1841, was *The Three Fishes*, being changed to *The Plough* in about 1870.

The Queen Adelaide, Kingston Road, was first mentioned in a directory for 1839. Since then it has been known as *The Adelaide Inn* and *The Adelaide Arms*, but the old name is now restored.

Thomas Pocock recalls that 'at the rear were stables and cowshed, plus a field at the side and rear where the landlord kept a few cows, made butter and sold skimmed milk to locals from the village.' The present building dates from 1932.

The Lord Nelson, High Street. The first mention of a pub on this site is in 1839 when it formed part of a terrace of small 18th- and 19th-century cottages. The name *Lord Nelson* first appears in the records in 1871. Before that it was referred to as a beerhouse or beer shop, with no name being given. In the 1851 Census the publican was Frederick Herring. By 1861 he was described as a 'beerhouse and cow keeper.' There was at that time ample grazing close at hand. The building was rebuilt at the turn of the century and demolished in 1963 to make way for Barclays Bank and a row of shops.

The Wheatsheaf, facing across Kingston Road to the River Hogsmill, was built in 1858.

There was previously a beerhouse on the site dating from the 1840s and called *King William IV*, which must have led to some confusion with the more conspicuous pub in the High Street.

The Mason's Arms, West Street, was a beerhouse that seems to have had a singularly short life. James Moore, a bricklayer, is recorded in the rate book of 1841 as occupier of *The Mason's Arms* and he appears in the 1845 directory as a beer retailer. Although he seems to have occupied the premises for about 25 years there are no other references to beer retailing. The house was situated opposite the National Schools.

83 *The Queen Adelaide* public house, c 1920. At the rear were stables and a cowshed.

84 *The Queen Adelaide* in 1999.

85 *The Lord Nelson* before demolition in 1963. It had been built *c.*1900.

The Brick Burner, London Road, was opened as a beerhouse in about 1850 and was much used by the workers at W.R. Waghorn's brick and tile works across the road. It was large enough to take in lodgers. By 1871 the name had been changed to *The Brick Kiln*. It ceased to be a pub in 1955 and for a period was a meeting place for the Jehovah's Witnesses before becoming a private dwelling.

The Jolly Waggoners, Beggars Hill, was built in the 1960s. It replaced a pub that was described in 1930 as having been 'originally a small ale-house behind a hedge' which dated from about 1850 and became a favourite resort of workers from the flour mills, and carters who watered their horses in the trough at the end of the half-moon pull-in.

The Star, Cheam Road, was a mid-19th-century building, which existed as a beerhouse for about 100 years. It was fairly commodious for in 1881 there were 17 persons present on Census night, including landlord, David Edwards, his wife and four children and 10 lodgers (all agricultural labourers).

The beerhouse closed in 1967 and half of the building became The Ewell Wine Stores while the other half was incorporated into the adjoining property, No. 31 High Street, to form a wine bar. No. 31 High Street is a timber-framed building, dating from the late 16th century. Before becoming a wine bar it was successively a dwelling house, a draper's shop, a chemist's and post office, a bank and lastly an antiques shop.

In 1998 the wine bar reverted to being a pub and the name was changed back to *The Star*. The pub incorporates the whole of the original *Star*.

The Glyn Arms, Cheam Road, was built in 1854, a few years after the opening of the Epsom and Croydon Railway, and was then called *The Railway Hotel*. When gas lighting came to Ewell in 1859 it marked the limit of the street lighting in this direction. At the turn of the century the pub used to have a small pull-in with a horse trough and was used mostly by carters, farm workers and, on Sundays, by people out walking for pleasure. By 1874 the name had been changed to *The Glyn Arms* (the Rev. Sir George Glyn being the ground land-lord). Later the inn sign showed the arms of the Glyns of Gaunts, the Dorset branch of the family, who succeeded to the Ewell baronetcy on the death of Sir Arthur Glyn. The building has been much altered in recent years and subject to changes of name.

The Organ Inn, London Road, originally faced directly on to the London Road, with a pull-in for carts and vans. It was rebuilt in its present position when the by-pass was made in the 1930s. The inn was a favoured resort for walkers from London, when Ewell was a village in the country, and it was the starting point on occasions for the local hunt. In 1998 it became Jim Thompson's Oriental Emporium (and Restaurant).

86 *The Star* incorporating a late 16th-century timber-framed building in 1999.

Chapter Eleven

The Glyns after 1800

Sir George Glyn, the second baronet, who is referred to in Part 1, died in 1814 and was outlived by his widow Dame Catherine by 30 years.

Sir Lewen Powell Glyn, 1801-40, the 3rd Baronet

Lewen Powell Glyn was only 13 years of age when his father died, and a legal document had to be drawn up admitting him to the estates. Other documents show that he was appointed a Cornet (2nd Lieutenant) in the Royal Dragoons and became a Lieutenant in 1824. He does not appear in later army lists.

It seems that Lewen Powell Glyn did not spend much time in Ewell. It is known that in 1835 he was living with his mother Dame Catherine in Bath. She had lived there before her marriage and her father was still living there. Lewen Powell died of epilepsy in a private asylum at Batheaston, a village just outside Bath, in 1840 at the age of 38 and was buried in the churchyard at Batheaston. When his mother died four years later she was laid in the same grave.

The Rev. Sir George Lewen Glyn, 1804-85

Of the seven Glyn baronets who were associated with Ewell it is the 4th, Sir George Lewen Glyn, who made the greatest impact. He studied for the Church and was appointed vicar of Ewell in 1831, the appointment being made by his brother, the 3rd baronet, who as holder of the Rectory Estate could appoint the vicar.

The Rev. George was responsible for commissioning plans for a new Rectory House which was completed in 1839 and is now known as Glyn House. St Mary's Church, a building dating largely from the 13th century, was in a poor state of repair: the 15th-century tower was in such bad condition that it was unsafe to ring the bells. George Glyn, now Sir George, having succeeded to the title in 1840 when his brother died, offered a plot of land and £500 towards the cost of a new church, provided that it could be built farther from the rectory than the old church. The result was the present St Mary's, built in the Gothic Revival style by Henry Clutton of Hartswood.

In 1838 George Glyn married, and his wife Emily née Birch gave him a son and two daughters. When Emily died, Sir George remarried at the age of 55, his new bride, Henrietta Amelia, a cousin, being 24 years younger than he. From this union came five children, three sons and two daughters.

The Rev. Sir George worked hard to bring the light to Ewell. In 1841 he had reported that the flour and gunpowder mills were obstacles because they worked on Sundays. He was happy to be able to record that there was less Sunday trading in shops than formerly, but the Epsom Races were a great source of perpetual demoralisation.

In 1866 Sir George took Henrietta to Russia, accompanied by his son and daughter by his first wife. It was an adventurous trip for those times, and took them to St Petersburg

87 The Rev. Sir George Glyn in 1864, painted by
Arthur Miles.

88 The Rectory in 1867, from a water-colour
painting.

89 Glyn House, formerly The Rectory, in 1992.

90 Glyn House taken in 1999 from the old church tower, illustrating how close The Rectory was to the old church.

91   The Rev. Sir George Glyn with his second wife
Henrietta and their children, Anna, Gervas, Margaret,
William Lewen (in the arms of nursemaid Mary
Williams), together with Emily, Sir George's daughter
by his first wife.

92   Henrietta Amelia Glyn in 1864, painted by Arthur
Miles.

93 Anna after her return from a trip to the Holy Land. Sadly, she died young after having teeth extracted under chloroform.

94 William Lewen, who went into the army, and died of meningitis at Malta at the age of 21.

and Moscow, while their return journey included stops in Finland, Sweden and Norway.

The Glyns arranged many social occasions for the parishioners: there were suppers for groups such as teachers, Sunday School teachers and the Mothers' Society and school treats. There were dinner parties for the Glyns' own strata of society attended by the owners of most of the local big houses.

It would seem that there was a genuine regard and affection for Sir George. An 'in memoriam' notice on his death in 1885 refers to him as

> Ewell's faithful Vicar, its generous Benefactor, its best Friend, its chief moving spirit and this for nearly half a century. We miss the venerable form that used to come in and out among us and we lament its loss, but we call to mind and love to dwell on his firm loving trust in his Saviour, his fine Christian character with its simplicity and sincerity, and genial kindness, the readiness to enter on whatever work concerned the well-being of his beloved Parish and the fixedness of purpose with which he would carry out such an object, labouring for it and never losing sight of it till it was accomplished; of which the Church, the National School and the Chapel at the Hamlet are enduring memorials.

The children of the Rev. Sir George Glyn

On the death of the Rev. Sir George, George Turbervil Glyn, his son by his first wife Emily Jane, became the 5th baronet in 1885. Little is known about him except that he was incapacitated by some mental disorder. When in 1891 he died a bachelor and intestate at a house at Richmond Hill at the age of 50, Sir Gervas Powell Glyn became the 6th baronet.

Of the two daughters by Sir George's first wife, one died as a young child: the other, Emily, married a bank manager and went to live in Somerset. Anna Lydia Glyn, the first of Sir George's children by his second wife, was a lively, high-spirited girl and had two novels published, one of which, *A Pearl of the Realm*,

95 Gervas, William Lewen and Arthur.

96 Arthur Glyn and companion.

is a romance of the Civil War period with scenes set in Ewell Village and Nonsuch Palace. Sadly, Anna did not live to see her book published. On 4 November 1895 she had 11 teeth extracted under chloroform and on 12 December 1895 aged 35 she died at the Rectory from heart failure.

Sir Gervas Powell Glyn was educated at Winchester and Oxford. He travelled widely in Europe and also Ceylon, India, China, Australia and many other parts of the world. Music was the main recreation of Gervas Powell Glyn: he played the cello and collected foreign and antique musical instruments, an interest he shared with his sister Margaret, who was three years younger than he. Until shortly after 1900 Gervas took an active part in local affairs as a member of the Parish Council and also served on the Epsom Rural District Council. Then he had what has been referred to as a mental breakdown and remained in poor health thereafter, dying in 1921.

William Lewen Glyn, the fourth child of Henrietta Amelia, went into the army after Cheam School and Winchester College. He was posted to Malta as a lieutenant in the 1st Battalion of the Dorsetshire Regiment and died there of meningitis at the age of 21.

Sir Arthur Glyn, 1870-1942, the 7th Baronet

Arthur Robert Glyn was the last child of Henrietta, the second wife of the 66-year-old Sir George Glyn. He was educated at Winchester and Cambridge. He never married.

Throughout his life Arthur Glyn was active in public affairs and headed many local organisations. In fact, he was well known throughout the county; his appointments included being a County Alderman, Chairman of Surrey Elementary Education Committee and a J.P. Education and young people were important to him and he loved to entertain them at Rectory House, accompany them on

97 Sir Arthur, who became the 7th and last Ewell Glyn baronet in 1921. He made a big contribution to local life and was popular with everyone.

rambles and sight-seeing tours of London and visit their schools. His interest extended beyond schooldays, and he was President of the Ewell Old Boys Association.

As a member of Surrey Education Committee for 20 years, Arthur Glyn made it his business to visit every school in the county. He supported and encouraged Epsom County School for Boys from its foundation in 1927 and in 1929 became first Chairman of the newly formed Board of Governors. His services were recognised when the school was renamed Glyn Grammar School in 1953 following a re-organisation of secondary education. It is now known simply as Glyn School.

As President of the Epsom and Ewell branch of the Lest We Forget Association he played a prominent part in helping disabled

ex-servicemen and arranged parties for them at Rectory House, which he also made available as the venue for local sports shows, flower shows and country dancing displays. The Ewell Band practised in the music room. Many local organisations held their annual general meetings at Rectory House. Arthur and Margaret Glyn lived in the Well House in Church Street, a pair of houses made into one and since separated again.

Arthur Glyn became Sir Arthur, the 7th baronet, in 1921, when he was 51, on the death of his brother Gervas. With habitual modesty he once remarked that 'he did not see why he should be a baronet: but for the fact that an ancestor gave assistance to an impecunious monarch he would have been plain Mr. Glyn'.

A typical reminiscence given by an elderly Ewell inhabitant was of being taken up to London for the day by Sir Arthur as a prize for winning a cricket competition:

> He was well known in London and many people spoke to him. As we walked past the Horse Guards, they saluted with their swords and Sir Arthur said to me, 'You liked that, didn't you ?' 'Yes, I did.' So he turned round and walked back again and they saluted again! He took me into a restaurant and said 'This young man would like some tea and lots of cream cakes'.

The favourite relaxation of Arthur Glyn was walking, and his visits to local schools and hospitals would be on foot. He would walk to meetings in Kingston. He died in January 1942 from pleurisy after catching a chill.

Among the many tributes the one from James Chuter Ede probably best sums up how local people felt about Sir Arthur Glyn:

> Ewell has lost one whose unselfish devotion was rendered so naturally, so unobtrusively and so continuously that it is no exaggeration to say we shall not see his like again ... he certainly never made an enemy, his friends were as numerous as the people with whom he came into contact.

Margaret, the last of the Glyns of Ewell

Margaret Henrietta Glyn, the second daughter of the second wife of Sir George Glyn, was born in 1865. She showed an aptitude for music and studied the organ, violin and viola, becoming a specialist in early English keyboard music. Although music was her over-riding passion she had many other activities that included in her youth horse riding and sailing. She took holidays on the Continent that would have been considered daring at the time.

Local history also received the attention of Margaret Glyn. There is in existence a document giving an account of the land holdings in Ewell in 1408 and when a transcription of it was published in 1913 she contributed a study relating the holdings to Ewell as it was at that later date and a conjectural map of medieval Ewell that has been widely consulted by modern historians.

When an attractive part of the parish, Hatch Furlong, was threatened by the proposed by-pass in the 1920s, it was Margaret Glyn who organised the opposition that tried to save it. She was instrumental in saving the grounds of Bourne Hall from developers.

After the death of her brother Arthur in 1942, the Rectory passed to Margaret Glyn and she sold it to Surrey County Council on generous terms. It has been renamed Glyn House and converted into a centre for educational conferences.

There are other tangible reminders of Margaret Glyn: a book that she wrote on Elizabethan music was an important and influential contribution to musical literature and her compositions included six symphonics, six orchestral suites, two overtures, organ music and many songs. Her crowning musical triumph was in 1945 when she was initiated as a Bard at the Welsh Eisteddfod following a

98 Anna and Margaret.

99 Margaret, who obtained a degree in music and became a competent composer.

100 The old Malt House in Church Street that Margaret Glyn purchased and converted into a music room and a museum for a collection of antique musical instruments.

101 The Malt House Museum. The collection was dispersed after the death of Margaret Glyn.

performance of her sixth symphony by the Liverpool Philharmonic Orchestra.

In 1908 Margaret Glyn purchased the Old Malt House in Church Street, Ewell, and had it converted into a music room and a museum for a collection of antique musical instruments. A few years ago, elderly inhabitants of Ewell recalled attending concerts of early music in the Malt House, presided over by Miss Glyn wearing a magnificent gown of silk brocade and looking extremely aristocratic. This was in marked contrast to her normal daytime dress that usually looked as if she had just left a dirty job in the garden.

A fellow enthusiast for Elizabethan music was the Welshman Leigh Vaughan Henry, who was an administrator and pianist as well as a composer. He was also known as a music critic and editor of music publications. His association with Margaret Glyn led to his visiting Ewell on numerous occasions. It is unclear whether or not Margaret Glyn's relationship with Leigh Henry went beyond musical collaboration, although there has been talk of a volume of love poems that he dedicated

to her. There was undoubtedly a close involvement and she left him the bulk of her considerable estate.

After Margaret Glyn died on 3 June 1946 at the age of 81, there was a court action in which the validity of codicils made to her will was challenged by one of the executors. It was stated that they had been written down by Leigh Henry while being dictated by Miss Glyn, and that she was completely infatuated with him. Mr. Justice Hodson gave judgment in favour of Leigh Henry in May 1948, saying he was satisfied that Miss Glyn was at the time of sound mind and knew and approved the contents of the codicils. Margaret, the last of the Ewell Glyns, was buried on 6 June 1946 in an earthen grave made near the entrance to the Glyn family vault near the site of the altar of the old church.

Margaret Glyn's music has been largely neglected since her death. Some amends were made on 5 October 1996 when several of her compositions were played at a concert in St Mary's Church, Ewell, to commemorate the 50th anniversary of her death.

Chapter Twelve

Local Government

Before well into the 19th century, local government really was local. Initially, matters of administration, registration of ownership of property and maintenance of law and order were the responsibility of the lord of the manor and the manorial court, aided from the mid-14th century onwards by Justices of the Peace appointed by the Crown.

However, people would meet in the vestry of the parish church to discuss problems and eventually by the 17th century Parliament made these vestry meetings responsible for matters such as the upkeep of local roads and bridges and the care of the poor and orphans as required by the Poor Laws.

The Ewell Vestry met at least four times a year and the wide range of matters they discussed is revealed by the minutes of these meetings. One of the most important jobs of the Vestry was the appointment of parish officers, including constables, waywardens, overseers of the poor, churchwardens and beadles. The Vestry was also responsible for setting the rates and arranging for their collection.

Keeping the peace was the concern of the Vestry and at a meeting on 23 April 1807 there was a complaint 'that several boys belonging to the Parish behave in a Riotous Manner in several parts of the Town and on Sundays in Particular'. It was recommended that 'the Constables and other Parish Officers will endeavour all they can to suppress such behaviour in future'. In 1853 the Commissioners of Police were requested to establish a Police Station in some central position in the Town of Ewell as under the present arrangements of the men living in private houses there is great difficulty and delay in procuring the aid of a policeman in sudden emergencies.

The request was not accepted, and to this day Ewell does not have a permanently manned police station.

Pest control was also the responsibility of the Vestry, and on 1 May 1828 it was resolved that in future the churchwardens would pay two pence per dozen for sparrows.

Rowdy bell ringers were sometimes a problem and on 25 June 1857,

It was Resolved that the Vicar and Churchwardens be requested to take such measures as in their judgement may be deemed necessary for organising the Bellringers and for bringing them under proper control.

It led to the drafting of 'Rules to be observed by the Company of Ringers' in August 1857. The object was to give the vicar and churchwardens control of bell ringing and included the provision that the bells could be rung only with their permission. Drinking and smoking in the belfry were subject to a fine of sixpence, and swearing and bad language two-pence. Bell ringers probably considered that the importance of their services merited a degree of independence. In the belfry of St Mary's is the legend: 'We to the Church the living call, and to the Grave do summon all'.

The arrival of the railways brought arguments with the railway companies over fair rates reflected in a minute of 11 January 1849 that 'Mr. Hall, on behalf of the Brighton & S.C. Railway Company, do protest against the assessment of the Company and inquired on what principle the assessment was made'. The matter required the setting up of a committee and reference to the Quarter Sessions before a settlement was reached in 1851 whereby a rateable value of £300, covering the line, land under cultivation and the station, was agreed.

The Vestry took an interest in the provision of amenities and on 27 October 1807 'It was agreed that a Lamp should be erected opposite the King's Head and that Thomas Goldsmith shall receive One Guinea Per Year for finding Oil and lighting the same'.

Nationally, growing populations and the overcrowded housing conditions associated with the Industrial Revolution brought about widespread bad health and disease. Epidemics of cholera swept through urban populations following the arrival of the disease from Asia in 1831. An outcome of the situation was the Public Health Act of 1848 which set up a General Board of Health as a central authority with the power to create local boards of health around the country.

In 1849 Ewell's neighbour, Epsom, was a much bigger town than Ewell. Overcrowding and the lack of main drains led to epidemics of typhoid and cholera. The General Board of Health was petitioned to take action, and the result was an official enquiry that led to the setting up of a Local Board of Health for Epsom in 1850. The Board got to work and organised a main drainage system and a piped water supply.

Ewell and Epsom had been drawn together in 1836 as two of the parishes in the Epsom Poor Law Union which came into being in that year and comprised some 15 parishes. Sanitary Authorities were established by a Public Health Act of 1875 with responsibility for sewage, drainage, street cleansing and water supply. Ewell and Cuddington became part of the Epsom Rural Sanitary District, with certain other parishes in the Epsom Poor Law Union.

Epsom town, having its own Board of Health, was not part of the Rural Sanitary Authority.

The Urban District Council of Epsom that was created in 1894 took over from the Epsom Board of Health. At the same time an Epsom Rural District Council was set up and this took over the responsibilities of the Epsom Rural Sanitary Authority.

Local government was scrutinised in 1933 and by the Surrey Review Order the Epsom Rural District Council was abolished, its responsibilities being shared among neighbouring authorities. The old parish of Ewell, most of Cuddington and bits of other parishes were given to the Epsom Urban District Council, which in consequence asked for its name to be changed to Epsom and Ewell Urban District Council.

The enlarged authority had sufficient confidence to ask for its status to be raised to that of a borough with its own corporation, and this honour was conferred. The official granting of the Charter of Incorporation by 'His Most Excellent Majesty King George VI' was on 29 September 1937, the presentation being made by 'His Majesty's Lieutenant of Surrey, Colonel The Right Honourable Lord Ashcombe'. It was an occasion for celebration, rejoicing and the display of civic pride.

The Charter Mayor was James Chuter Ede and his procession of 10 carriages left the recently built town hall at 8.50 a.m. for a parade through the borough to Nonsuch Park where they awaited the arrival of the Lord Lieutenant. They proceeded to the Mansion House in Nonsuch Park, where various dignitaries were presented to the Lord Lieutenant. The 10 carriages and their distinguished occupants then returned to the Clock Tower, Epsom, via a circuitous route that took in Ewell High Street and many other roads in the northern part of the Borough.

Music was provided by the Band of the 9th Queen's Royal Lancers that played at the Clock Tower in the morning and at Nonsuch Park in the afternoon. At the presentation

102 The new Town Hall was completed in time for the incorporation of Epsom and Ewell in 1937.

103 The Charter Mayor, James Chuter Ede, receives the Charter from the Lord Lieutenant of Surrey, Colonel The Right Honourable Lord Ashcombe.

ceremony that took place on a dais by the Clock Tower at 12 noon, 16 trumpeters sounded fanfares.

A Guard of Honour was provided by the 318th Anti-Aircraft Company of the Royal Engineers (T.A.) and the 5th Battalion of the East Surrey Regiment. After the presentation ceremony there was a civic luncheon in the Members' Luncheon Room of the Grand Stand, Epsom Downs.

The programme of events to celebrate Epsom and Ewell becoming a borough included two Charter Balls held in the Grand Stand and fairs in local recreation grounds. There was also an historical pageant through the streets of the Borough and an open air dance in Rosebery Park; numerous buildings were floodlit. The Charter Mayor, accompanied by Members and Officers of the Council and representatives of local organisations, attended a civic service at Epsom Parish Church on Sunday 3 October.

Many local inhabitants and others interested in the municipality presented commemorative gifts to the Corporation, ranging from a mace of the corporation, given by James Chuter Ede,

to the mayor's robe and hat given by the elementary schoolchildren of the borough.

The granting of the charter was not the only ceremony that took place on 29 September 1937. At 4.20 p.m. the Lord Lieutenant, the Charter Mayor and the Civic contingent returned to the Mansion House, Nonsuch Park, for the official opening of the Park by Lord Snell, Chairman of the London County Council.

The relationship between Epsom and Ewell has reversed over the years. In 1618 Epsom was only a small village but Ewell was a small town that had been granted a licence to hold a market. The discovery of Epsom Salts, reputedly in 1618, led to the rapid expansion of Epsom as visitors came to take the waters. By 1690 it was sufficiently well-established as a spa to justify building the assembly rooms now known as Waterloo House. Although by about 1740 Epsom's days as a spa were over, the town continued to attract well-to-do people because of the races. There was racing on the Downs at an early date—it was one of the entertainments

104 The ceremony of granting the Charter of Incorporation to Epsom and Ewell took place in front of the clock tower in Epsom High Street on 29 September 1937.

associated with the spa, and it was given a great boost when two new races, the Oaks and the Derby, were inaugurated in 1779 and 1780. The result was that Epsom grew faster than Ewell. By 1891 Epsom parish had a population of over 8,000 while that of Ewell was only about 2,500 and it would have been considered a village rather than a town.

It is really a story of Ewell progressively losing its independence to Epsom from 1836. Although in 1894 Ewell was given its own parish council, its powers were confined to minor issues, and of course the parish council lasted only until 1933 when it was taken over by Epsom Urban District Council. From that date Ewell no longer had a separate identity from the administrative point of view: the old

parish falls within the present-day Ruxley, Cuddington, Ewell Court, Auriol, Stoneleigh, Nonsuch, West Ewell and Ewell Wards of the Borough of Epsom and Ewell.

With regard to National Government, Epsom and Ewell have of necessity long been in similar situations. In the early days of Parliament there were only two Surrey members for the whole county. It is of interest that William Saunder of Ewell was a Surrey member from 1553 to 1555. After the reforms of 1832 Epsom and Ewell came in the West Surrey constituency and after more recent changes of constituency boundaries the whole of Epsom and Ewell plus Ashtead Common, Ashtead Park, Ashtead Village, Nork, Preston and Tattenhams are served by one member.

Chapter Thirteen

The Railway and Public Utilities

The Railway

Railways developed rapidly after the successful opening of the Liverpool to Manchester line in 1830. In the south east by 1850 there was a network of lines radiating from London, including the London & Brighton Railway Company line to Brighton which opened as early as 1841. The route was London Bridge, New Cross, Norwood, Croydon, Redhill, Horley, Three Bridges, Haywards Heath and Brighton.

The London & Croydon Railway Company had plans to extend its lines from Croydon to Epsom and these were well advanced by 27 July 1846 when it was amalgamated with the London & Brighton Railway Company to form the London, Brighton & South Coast (LBSC) Railway. The Epsom line with a station at East Ewell was opened on 10 May 1847. It was to have been operated as an atmospheric railway. This was a system on which the train had no locomotive; instead it was propelled by a piston travelling in a continuous iron tube 15 inches in diameter laid between the tracks. The piston was sucked along the tube by exhausting the air by means of stationary engines installed in pumping houses situated at intervals along the track. Early trials had indicated that the system was successful, but experience showed that there were insuperable practical difficulties attached to its widespread use and work on the Epsom atmospheric railway was halted in December 1846. The line was completed as a conventional steam railway.

In the early days, the London terminus for the London, Brighton & South Coast Railway was London Bridge. Victoria Station was not opened until 1860, after the building of the Grosvenor Bridge to take the railway over the river. At various times the bridge had to be widened to take additional tracks.

105 Ewell East Station before the down-line platform buildings and canopy were demolished.

106 Ewell West Station in 1999, largely unchanged since its early days.

The original route to Epsom was via Croydon and Waddon. A more direct route became available in 1868 when a new line from Peckham Rye to Sutton that included Mitcham Junction, Hackbridge and Carshalton was opened.

Ewell acquired its West Ewell station on 4 April 1859 when the Wimbledon to Epsom line opened on what was soon to become the London & South Western Railway.

Originally, the Croydon-Epsom line through East Ewell terminated in an engine shed at the beginning of what is now the Upper High Street, Epsom, with the station nearby: a station building is still there, now largely hidden by shops. Then the LBSC Railway negotiated joint use of the LSW Railway tracks beyond Epsom and a short line was built crossing East Street by a bridge to link the two systems. However, the station in the Upper High Street continued in use until 1929, by which time both companies were part of the Southern Railway.

Water

One of the first major tasks of the Epsom Local Board of Health which was established in 1850 was to provide a public water supply. They purchased the site of an artesian well in East Street in 1853 and began laying mains through-out the parish of Epsom. Ewell had to wait until the Sutton District Water Company was authorised to supply it in 1871. Ewell still gets its water from the company which in 1996 became part of Sutton and East Surrey Water. It had started life in 1863 as the Sutton & Cheam Water Company. Water is pumped from wells sunk into the chalk. There are several covered high-level storage reservoirs, including one constructed at North Looe in 1960.

Although the Sutton District Water Company was authorised to supply water to Ewell in 1871, mains water did not reach some of the cottages for many years. A report prepared in 1895 covering 248 cottages said that only 116 of them were supplied from mains, the occupants of the remainder having to collect their water from stand-pipes or wells. Only 12 of the cottages had WCs with a proper water supply, while 69 had to make do with open privies or middens and 82 used earth closets with pails.

Sewerage

The Epsom Rural Sanitary Authority that had been set up following the Act of 1875 was responsible for providing a system of drains for Ewell. However, it was not until 1894 that the Authority got round to inviting engineers to submit estimates for effectively draining and disposing of sewage in Ewell. (The Local Government Act of 1894 set up the Epsom

Rural District Council, which had its first meeting on 8 January 1895 and took over the responsibilities of the Sanitary Authority.) The project was not without its problems, in particular regarding the site of the outfall plant (sewage treatment works). The preferred site was on Ruxley Farm, but the landowner, Mr. A.W. Gadesden, objected on the grounds that it was near a cowhouse fitted for 40 cows and also the farmhouse. He proposed a site farther from the farm. As the alternative site would have made the scheme more expensive, the Authority applied for powers to acquire the preferred site by compulsory purchase, but they were not supported by the central Local Government Board. This led to a resolution from Ewell Parish Council in March 1897 regretting that the well meant endeavours to provide Ewell with a system of drainage had been frustrated.

There were further negotiations with Mr. Gadesden regarding the alternative site, but progress was so slow that in January 1899 the Clerk of the Committee (by then the Rural District Council) was instructed to call again the attention of the Local Government Board to the long delay in this matter and to state that the same was considered a public scandal! In March 1899 it was agreed to submit amended plans for Ewell drainage to the Local Government Board, together with a request for a

sanction to borrow £18,200 to pay for the scheme. The Board accepted the proposals and in July 1899 tenders from contractors were being received—that from a Wolverhampton firm was accepted. There was soon a need to increase the loan to £23,000 because of the exceptional nature of the work near the Ewell springs necessitating a considerable amount of pumping.

The final plans used for the drainage were by J. Beasley and Son and Nicholls and involved the construction of a 15-inch main sewer from the outfall north of Ruxley Farm to the centre of Ewell village (the High Street/Church Street junction), with 12-inch and 9-inch branch pipes that extended the system as far as *The Glyn Arms*, Half Mile Bush (Epsom Road), Gibraltar, West Ewell, Ruxley Lane/Kingston Road, *The Queen Adelaide*, Bankside (where Rembrandt Cinema was later built, and London Road (near Stoneleigh House). The work was completed in 1901.

In June 1900 it had been agreed that lateral drains would be laid from the sewers to the boundary of each house in Ewell, some 400 connections in all, and extra money had to be borrowed to cover this.

The Ruxley sewage treatment works were in operation until after the completion in 1957 of the Hogsmill Valley Sewage Works at Lower Marsh Lane, Kingston and the laying of sewers to bring the sewage to the new works.

107 Pumping work in progress near the *Spring Hotel* c.1900, when main drains were installed.

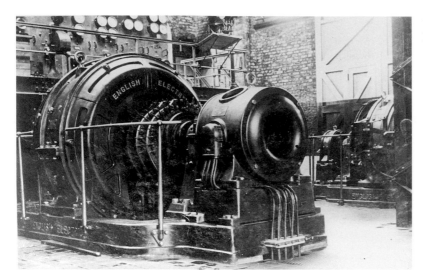

108 Rotary convertors in Epsom Power Station in the 1930s.

Gas

Ewell acquired gas soon after Epsom: the Epsom and Ewell Gas Company was set up in 1839 'for the purpose of lighting with gas the towns of Epsom and Ewell'. The capital of the company was £3,000 in £10 shares. There was a singular lack of enthusiasm among the shareholders in the early days and the minute books show that on several occasions a sufficient number of share-holders did not attend to constitute a meeting! On 25 August 1841 it was reported that the gas-works were imperfect and inadequate and the directors were authorised to buy new machinery. By 1912 there were three gasholders on the site in East Street, Epsom. In 1913 the supply was taken over by the Wandsworth Gas Company and the East Street works ceased production in 1933. However, they were brought back into use in the Second World War to produce hydrogen for barrage balloons, which was stored in the gasholders. The fire-watchers at the site had an unenviable task: it would have needed more than a few stirrup pumps and buckets of sand to deal with a fire there.

Electricity

Epsom Urban District Council set up a generating station in Depot Road which began to supply electricity on 5 February 1902. The station was powered by steam and had a capacity of 110 kW. More steam-driven plant was installed in 1904 and 1906, but extensions in 1913 and subsequent ones employed diesel engines.

The original Board of Trade authorisation for Epsom excluded Ewell, but an Extension Order of 1917 included it, so a public supply of electricity would have come to Ewell during 1918-19. Some of the big houses had their own generators before that date, for instance, a 1917 catalogue for Ewell Castle shows an engine house equipped with a 12 h.p. oil engine, dynamo, and 48 chloride battery cells. By 1923 Ewell Castle was taking its electricity from the mains.

The supply from the Epsom Electricity Undertaking was direct current. In 1930 the Undertaking began to take an alternating current supply from the London and Home Counties Joint Electricity Authority, and the Epsom generators were thereafter used mainly for standby purposes. However, the a.c. supply was converted to d.c. for local consumers by means of rotary convertors at the Depot Road premises and mercury arc rectifiers at various sub-stations throughout the area. This equipment was progressively taken out of use as there was conversion to an a.c. system. The Epsom and Ewell Electricity Undertaking was in being until nationalisation in 1948.

Chapter Fourteen

The River Hogsmill and its Mills

The character of Ewell owes a great deal to its little river, the Hogsmill, that rises in springs in the village and flows in a generally north-west direction before joining the Thames at Kingston, a course of some seven miles. The name 'Hogsmill' is believed to have come from John Hogg, a Kingston miller around 1200.

The ponds associated with the river, particularly those by Bourne Hall and Ewell Court, and grassy open spaces along it, give the area a great deal of charm. The main stream is joined by tributaries, some within the parish of Ewell and others nearer Kingston, that augment the flow. However, water from the springs was sufficiently copious for several mills to be operated close to the source; these included the Ewell Upper and Lower Mills and the Gunpowder Mills.

The spring water came from aquifers in the chalk of the North Downs, and records for the period 1879-85 gave a mean flow equivalent to 27.3 megalitres per day at the Lower Mill. In recent years the flow has drastically reduced because of increased extraction of water from the chalk by water companies and other users and for periods in the early 1990s Bourne

109 The River Hogsmill at Ruxley Splash, *c.*1910.

85

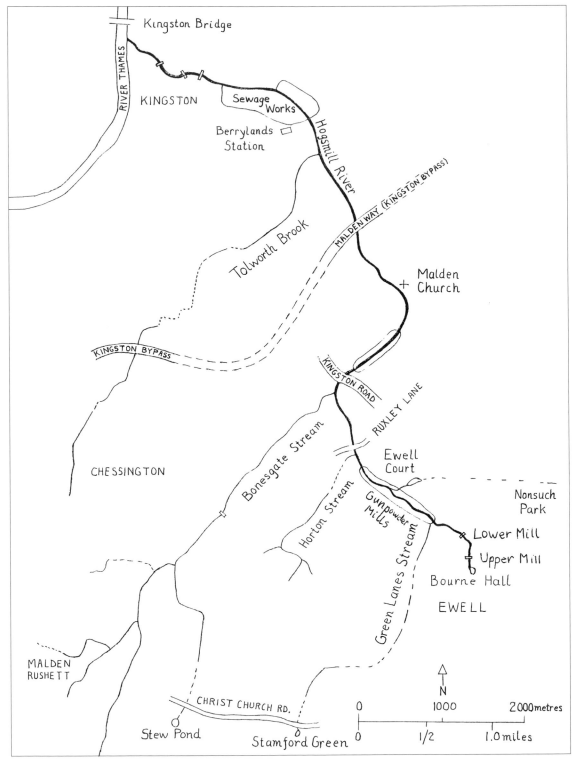

110 Map of the River Hogsmill.

Hall Lake was completely dry. This led to a deal in 1994 between the Environment Agency and Sutton & District Water Company whereby, in return for being allowed to pump water from a borehole in Nonsuch Park, the Water Company paid for the lake to be lined to retain water and a minimum flow of water maintained by pumping from a borehole near the Upper Mill.

The Upper Mill

The mill closest to the main source of the river below what is now Bourne Hall Lake is thought to be a mill referred to in the Domesday Survey. In medieval times it belonged to Fitznells' manor. There may have been as many as six pairs of stones at one time, but in the early 1900s there was only sufficient water to run three pairs of stones continuously; the supply continued to diminish until only one pair could be run, and not continuously, so that a gas engine had to be

111　A miller at work in the Upper Mill in the 1920s.

112　The Upper Mill in 1990 after 'restoration', a restoration so thorough that the mill lost its listed building status.

113 Lower Mill and Mill House, 1929. The mill was destroyed by fire in 1938, but the Mill House survived.

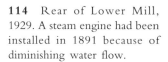

114 Rear of Lower Mill, 1929. A steam engine had been installed in 1891 because of diminishing water flow.

installed to drive the stones. By 1953 milling had become uneconomic and operation ceased. Epsom and Ewell Borough Council bought the building and there were hopes that it would be made available for community use. But the financial situation was unfavourable and the building was sold to developers for office accommodation. Although the mill today looks much as it did in earlier times, it was in fact virtually rebuilt, to the extent that it lost its listed building status.

The last miller was Mr. P.P. Henderson, whose great-grandfather, Charles Hall, had run the mill in partnership with a Mr. Davidson. For a period, Hall and Davidson ran both the Upper Mill and the Lower Mill.

The Lower Mill

The Lower Mill was not always just a corn mill. In 1732 William Jubb was operating it as a paper mill also. Later, it was rebuilt as a larger corn mill with three pairs of stones. As with the Upper Mill, there were problems with the diminishing flow of water and in 1891 a steam engine had to be installed. The opportunity was taken to modernise the mill and replace some of the stones with the steel rollers used to produce white flour. The mill went out of production in 1929 and had a period of light industrial use. In 1938 it was destroyed by fire; fortunately, the adjacent millhouse, parts of which date back to *c*.1600, survived, and was later converted to offices.

The Gunpowder Mills

In Victorian times the Ewell Gunpowder Mills were an important local industry: the 1871 census returns record 156 workers at the mills. They are believed to have been established on the site in 1754 by Alexander Bridges and Jonathan Eade and were operated by the Bridges family until 1861, when Sharpe, Adams and Company took over.

Gunpowder mills buildings were normally well spread out to minimise damage in the event of an explosion, and the Ewell mills were on a site of about 45 acres stretching along the river for some half a mile, starting approximately a quarter mile downstream of the Lower Mill.

The 1866 Ordnance Survey map indicates that there were at least three mill-wheels driving pairs of grindstones. Gunpowder making is a dangerous business and explosions were not infrequent: records show at least seven explosions at the Ewell mills. There was a particularly bad one in 1863, when three men were killed. In the words of Sir George Glyn, it was 'an awful catastrophe that scattered their bodies in mangled pieces over the adjoining fields'. There are graves of victims of explosions in the churchyard of St Mary's, Ewell. The Bridges family lived in Avenue House, the grounds of which adjoined the gunpowder mills site. The house was rebuilt in 1879, and is now known as Ewell Court, where there is a library and other community amenities. Although the house looks typical of a mansion of the period, at the centre, part of the earlier 17th-century building survives.

The mills closed in 1875, probably because the requirements of the Explosives Act of that year would have made them uneconomic and the site was soon cleared. There were further improvements in the 1950s when the land was landscaped as part of the 'Hogsmill Open Space', and a further step towards the creation of a public amenity was the making of the 'Hogsmill Walk', a nearly continuous path along the banks of the river from the Upper Mill, Ewell, to the River Thames at Kingston, which was formally opened in the spring of 1985. The mayor of Epsom and Ewell at that time, Councillor Norma Fryer, walked the path from Ewell to meet her counterpart from Kingston mid-way along the river. Her sensible dress that included an anorak and wellies made an unusual setting for the mayoral gold chain!

115 The Ewell Powder Mills following an explosion in 1863.

116 The last remaining mixing house of the powder mills, *c.*1900.

The Hogsmill and Navigation

There is no evidence that the river was used seriously for water transport. Being so dependent on springs, the flow would have been subject to wide seasonal variations so that at times there would have been insufficient depth of water for boats. Also, the numerous mills would have impeded navigation. However, this did not stop an 18th-century lord of the manor, Edward Northey, from ordering a survey to be carried out to estimate the expense of making the river navigable from Ewell to Kingston. Although the document that details the survey is undated, the names of owners of properties referred to suggest a date between 1755 and 1760.

The surveyors were a Mr. Nickals and a Mr. Broughton, and they presented their findings in a meticulous way, dividing the work into separate sections, and giving the cost with remarkable precision, as the following sample will show:

> To a lock compleated fit for service to render a communication of boats of upwards thirty tons burthen between the upper mill-head, viz Mr Challoner's Mill and the tail of the same ... considered as a ten foot head ... £550. 5s. ¾d.

The estimate covered other locks and a number of swing bridges and came to a total of £6,851 12s. 11d. It is not known why it was decided not to proceed with the scheme.

Ewell also featured in a later, much more ambitious waterway scheme, The Grand Imperial Ship Canal. In 1828 Parliament was asked to consider a bill for the construction of a ship canal from London to Portsmouth. What was proposed really was for ships, rather than for barges. It was to have been 150 feet wide and 28 feet deep and it would have enabled large ocean-going vessels to sail from Rotherhithe on the Thames to the English Channel. It would have had locks 300 feet long and 64 feet wide. The shortest of the possible routes went through the North Downs by means of the Mole Gap to Dorking, and would have passed across Epsom Common. Ewell would have been linked to the canal by a branch connection. The bill was rejected by the Government because it was not considered to be financially viable which was hardly surprising, as some of the cuttings that might have been necessary could have been as much as 250 feet deep!

Chapter Fifteen

The 20th Century until the Second World War

In spite of the many changes that came about in the 19th century, at the beginning of the 20th century Ewell was still largely a rural community with numerous farms and a few big houses lived in by the gentry who employed servants. The most dominant family were the Glyns. The biggest landowner was Augustus William Gadesden of Ewell Castle, who had inherited the three sub-manors of Ewell, but following his death in 1901 they were broken up for sale. The High Street with its shops was the focal point.

The First World War

When war was declared on 3 August 1914 few people realised just what type of war it was going to be. Field Marshal Sir John French was confident it would be over by Christmas. However, local men flocked to Epsom to join up. As early as December 1914, 159 Ewell men had enlisted. The war was not over by Christmas, and by 28 January 1916 men no longer had a choice: conscription was introduced for males aged from 18 to 40, and more and more Ewell men became involved.

117   Green Man Street (now High Street), *c*.1905.

Although the people who remained in Ewell were spared the bombing of the Second World War, things were difficult enough. As well as their men being away there were food shortages and rising prices to be coped with. In 1915 Income Tax was doubled, to 1s. 6d. on earned income and 2s. on unearned income.

The Ewell Parish Council minutes reflect war-time conditions, with frequent references to members of the armed forces being killed and wounded, or receiving decorations for gallantry. There seems to have been a problem with discharged Belgian soldiers who had been housed in the large house, Ewell Grove, and on 10 May 1915 an appeal was made that people should not treat them to drinks. In July 1918 arrangements were made for collecting fruit stones and nut shells for making charcoal to use in gas-masks. Although there was no bombing in Ewell in the First World War, London had been bombed, and the parish council discussed the need to extinguish street lights during possible air raids.

Ewell lost 80 men in the First World War and their names are recorded on the memorial by the Dipping Place and also on the memorial in the churchyard of the parish church.

118   1st Ewell Boy Scouts band outside St Mary's, *c*.1910.

119   Ewell Downs Motor Services was set up by Mr. John Swift on Reigate Road in 1929 opposite what is now the entrance to Sainsbury's Homebase.

120   When the bypass was built in 1932 it cut across Reigate Road by the side of Ewell Downs Motor Services, which could then have an entrance from the bypass, and more petrol pumps were installed.

121 Advertisement for houses on Nonsuch Park Estate.

122 Margaret Glyn organised a public meeting to oppose the Ewell bypass.

Between the Wars

After 1918 things changed rapidly, as the motor car began to take over the roads. Although the railway had come to Ewell in 1847 its most dramatic impact came after 1925 when it was electrified and services became more frequent. A new station at Stoneleigh encouraged the growth of housing estates and more and more farmland was built on (see Chapter 16). The Old Fair Field near the heart of Ewell Village was also the site of new roads and houses, a development that started in 1935. It was also in 1935 that the builders, Gleeson, bought Nonsuch Court Farm and began to build the Nonsuch Park Estate comprising some 30 residential roads between Cheam Road and Nonsuch Park on either side of the railway.

The Bypass

In the early 1930s a bypass was built to relieve the centre of Ewell from the ever-increasing flow of vehicles. It was a hotly contested issue, since the road proposed by Surrey County Council was to be taken through the attractive Hatch Furlong to the east of the village, which conservationists wanted to save. Margaret Glyn was particularly concerned: she had bought Hatch Furlong in 1911 to save it from development. In 1927 she conveyed the property to the National Trust, thinking that they would be better able to protect the land than an individual. However, when it appeared that extra effort was needed, Margaret Glyn started her own campaign and employed the Professor of Town Planning at London

University, S.D. Adshead, to give an opinion. The Professor proposed several alternative schemes, one of which would have taken the road past West Ewell Station, over Chessington Road into Pound Lane, along Waterloo Road and behind Epsom Station, alongside the railway line, eventually crossing it and coming out on the Dorking road, thus by-passing the centre of Epsom as well as the centre of Ewell.

While Professor Adshead carried out his investigation, Margaret Glyn went into action, writing letters to national as well as local newspapers and organising a public meeting. The result was a petition to Surrey County Council signed by nearly 1,200 people opposing the officially proposed route and backing the Adshead alternative. The petition was considered but the alternative route was rejected on the grounds that it was longer and more expensive than that being officially planned.

The Ministry of Transport supported Surrey County Council and the planned bypass went ahead, being officially opened in July 1932.

Margaret Glyn did succeed in having the Nonsuch Palace Banqueting House site made available to the people of Ewell in compensation for the destruction of Hatch Furlong. The Banqueting House site was not the only land acquired by the public in the 1930s. From the Stoneleigh development came the 18-acre Auriol Park and 25-acre Cuddington Recreation Ground (in Cheam). But a much more extensive acquisition was Nonsuch Park. Other open spaces that were made available are the gardens of Bourne Hall and those of Ewell Court.

A significant event in 1933 was the transfer of responsibility for Ewell from Epsom Rural District Council to Epsom Urban District Council, which four years later became Epsom and Ewell Borough Council (see Chapter 12).

123 The United Reformed Church in London Road was built in 1938 as a Congregational Church. The original Ewell Congregational Church had been built in 1864-5 in the High Street (or Green Man Street as that particular stretch of road was then called) on the plot of land that is now the Longhurst Memorial Garden.

Chapter Sixteen

Stoneleigh

Until the 1930s the area of Ewell now known as Stoneleigh was the open farmland of Worcester Park, Sparrow, Cold Harbour and Bowling Green Farms, which formed an estate that had been purchased by John Jeffries Stone from Felix Ladbrook in 1860. J.J. Stone died in 1879 and the estate passed to trustees who in 1930 were Walter Henry Stone, Ralph Browning Leckie Stone and Kenneth Walter Stone. It was known as the Stoneleigh Estate.

The arrival of the railway in 1859 with a station at Worcester Park had led to some development near the station by the Landed Estates Company. Detached houses built along The Avenue were serviced by workers who lived in smaller houses on an estate on the opposite side of the railway.

On the Stoneleigh Estate there was a small amount of development in the early 1900s when Park Avenue at the extreme southern end was built up, but in 1930 the area was still largely fields, farms and patches of woodland. It was not to be expected that such a rural region less than 15 miles from central London would much longer be able to withstand the pressures of the population explosion that was building up in north-west Surrey.

A major factor in that population growth was the electrification of the railways by the Southern Railway following its formation in 1923. They opted for a 660-volt direct current third-rail system rather than the higher voltage overhead conductor system used for some suburban electrification programmes. Installation of the new equipment went ahead rapidly and by the end of 1931 the S.R. had converted practically the whole of its suburban lines. Electric traction is much more flexible than steam traction. An electric locomotive goes as soon as it is switched on, unlike a steam engine that has to get up steam! The electric services were more frequent and faster; over the S.R. system as a whole, stations were served by more than twice as many trains as before. The line to Epsom through Worcester Park had been electrified as early as 1925, giving a service of three trains an hour.

The improved train service and the growing demand for houses made the Stoneleigh Estate ripe for development, and the trustees of J.J. Stone began selling off land.

Walter Hobbs purchased Sparrow and Worcester Park Farms and had plans to build 2,750 houses and a number of shops. The Epsom Rural District Council began to take an interest in the development and made an Interim Development Order covering something like 350 acres of Sparrow and Worcester Park Farms. There was provision for about 3,000 houses, a suitable number of shops and 24 acres of open space. In 1930 the Council's engineers began to plan the drains. Walter Hobbs sold plots of land to various builders and in 1931 work began on what was to become known as Stoneleigh Park. It was to be served by a new railway station, the building of which was agreed between the Southern Railway and the trustees of the late J.J. Stone, the latter agreeing to pay nearly half the cost and make the necessary land available free of charge.

The new station was about a mile and a quarter south of Worcester Park Station and a mile north of Ewell West Station. It was opened on 17 July 1932, and when first built it was surrounded by fields: the houses came later. There was to be a wide shopping street going off to the east (The Broadway), linked to residential roads that gave access to London Road. The six roads north of the Broadway and its extension, The Glade, were parallel to the railway and London Road. Like the other estate roads, they were narrow concrete roads with narrow grass verges and tarmac or gravel footways.

There was no road crossing the railway to link Stoneleigh Park to Stoneleigh Hill on the other side of the line, just a footbridge. The Broadway was soon developed as a shopping centre: by 1934 more than 30 shops were ready for use, including a sub-post office. There was a cake shop with tea room at the back which became a social centre. Further shops were erected in 1937 and in 1939. A branch of Midland Bank opened in 1934.

The area to the west of the station on the other side of the line was developed into what became known as the Stoneleigh Hill Estate by a company with that name. The first semis were on sale by the end of 1933. To the west of Stoneleigh Hill behind *The Queen Adelaide* public house on the site of Chesterfield House and its grounds, Ideal Homes built the Chesterfield Park Estate, where houses went on sale in 1935. To the north west of Chesterfield Park Estate on the same side of Kingston Road was built in 1934-7 the Davis Estate on the site of a Victorian house, Parkside, and its grounds. It had been a prep school.

On the other side of Kingston Road opposite *The Queen Adelaide* were built Ewell Court Estate and Ewell Court Farm Estate, while later came Ruxley Estate to the north west, consisting mainly of bungalows, developed between 1936 and 1939.

124 Stoneleigh railway station opened in July 1932. When first built it was surrounded by fields, with no houses.

125 One of the attractions offered in the Firswood Avenue houses on the Chesterfield Park Estate was a 'state of the art' fireplace with a built in clock and radio.

The area around Stoneleigh House which had given the district its name was developed as Ewell Park Estate.

The Broadway by Stoneleigh Station was not the only shopping complex: another grew up on both sides of the Kingston Road at the junction with Stoneleigh Park Road. By 1938 it had nearly fifty shops open. However, the claim of the Broadway as the main social centre was confirmed when, in 1934, a licence for a public house was granted and the impressive mock-Tudor *Stoneleigh Hotel* was built. It was opened on 4 November 1935 and in addition to the bars it had a billiard room and a large hall for meetings, receptions and dances. It quickly became the neighbourhood social centre, a popular meeting place for the young people of Ewell Village as well as the new Stoneleigh.

126 Stoneleigh Broadway, first phase of development.

127 Chesterfield House in 1909. It was demolished when the Chesterfield Park Estate was developed in 1934-5.

128 Mr. Geoffrey Abery with his new BSA motorcycle in Manor Drive on the Ewell Court Farm Estate in 1935.

129 Stoneleigh was named after the Stoneleigh Estate that had been acquired by J.J. Stone in 1860. He had Stoneleigh House built, seen here on an 1882 sales catalogue.

Further entertainment came on 3 October 1938 with the opening of the 1,500 seat Rembrandt cinema, adjacent to the Kingston Road shopping area. The ceremony was performed by the mayor of Epsom and Ewell and there were personal appearances by Will Hay, Graham Moffatt and Moore Marriott, a trio of comic actors popular at the time. Another celebrity present was Tom Walls, the actor and racehorse owner. During its early years the Rembrandt staged live shows as well as films—singers, pianists and on at least three occasions the London Philharmonic Orchestra, conducted by Basil Cameron, Richard Tauber and Sir Adrian Boult. In 1945 the Rembrandt was bought by Associated British Cinemas and in 1986 by Cannon Cinemas Ltd. It was demolished in 1998.

The religious needs of Anglicans were catered for by St John the Baptist Church, opened in May 1939, situated to the west of the railway station, following temporary accommodation from July 1936 in a small hall behind the Broadway shops. Baptists, Methodists and Roman Catholics also provided themselves with accommodation. Surrey County Council provided schools, the Stoneleigh East Council School and the Stoneleigh West School.

130   St John the Baptist Church, Stoneleigh, opened in May 1939, photographed in 1999.

Stoneleigh has developed as a suburb with a distinct identity, a situation that has been helped by a number of factors. The boundaries have been partly delimited by geographical features; there is Nonsuch Park and London Road to the south east, while south west there is old Ewell and the bypass. Politically, the division between Epsom and Ewell and Cheam, which came about as a consequence of the Surrey Review Order of 1933, has tended to define the northern boundary. But the major factor has been an active residents' association.

In his comprehensive account of the development of Stoneleigh in 'Semi-detached London', Alan Jackson concludes that, 'mercifully preserved from the worst excesses of modern motor traffic by its quaint road layout, Stoneleigh has evolved to a not unattractive, restful, maturity'.

Chapter Seventeen

The Second World War

By 1939 Ewell had lost much of its early identity and was so much a part of the Borough of Epsom and Ewell that an account of the impact of the Second World War has to be largely in terms of the borough.

The declaration of war at 11 a.m., Sunday, 3 September 1939, marked the beginning of nearly six years of disruption to normal life, six years of austerity, anxiety and drabness punctuated by moments of dread, horror and heartbreak. The war was not unexpected—for several years there had been preparations; an Air Raid Precaution organisation (A.R.P.) had been set up and air-raid shelters constructed. Gas masks had been issued.

The Black-out

The most immediate impact of the war on the people of Epsom and Ewell was having to cope with the black-out. It had been ordered that all lights that might be seen from the air and give guidance to enemy bombers must be obscured. The regulations were strictly enforced by the Police, the Special Police and Air Raid Wardens. If the cry 'put out that light' was ignored too often, the offender would end up in court.

Road vehicles had to mask their lights and only dim torches were allowed to help people find their way around the darkened streets. Although council workers had painted white bands around trees, lamp-posts and other obstacles, in the early months of the war the black-out caused far more work for the hospitals than did enemy action.

Air-raid Shelters

The provision of air-raid shelters proceeded apace. Some householders built their own in their cellars, garages or gardens, while others were pleased to accept the official issue Anderson Shelter. This was made up from corrugated iron sheets, some of them curved, so that when bolted together they formed a barrel-vaulted compartment 6½ feet long, 4½ feet wide and with maximum headroom of about 6 feet. It could accommodate six people sitting. The shelter was buried to a depth of four feet and covered with at least 15 inches of soil. The entrance was protected by a blast wall of sandbags, earth or bricks.

During 1939 some 3,500 Anderson Shelters were made available to householders in Epsom and Ewell, free of charge to those earning less than £250 per annum or at a charge of between £6 and £10 for better-off households. Also, some public shelters were built. M.J. Gleesons were contracted by the Borough Council in 1939 to build at various locations six large air-raid shelters made from pre-cast concrete panels. The biggest was in Rosebery Park and it would accommodate 1,440 persons. The ones in Ewell were near the bypass (540 persons), West Ewell between Chessington Road and the Horton Light Railway (180 persons) and at Ruxley near Riverview Road (180 persons). Large underground shelters included two on Epsom Downs, one near Buckle's Gap and the other between Ashley Road and Chalk Lane (1,500 persons). Public brick surface shelters were also built, including

131   A decontamination course held at Ewell Court under the instructions of Capt. E.C. Jervis, M.C., A.R.P. Organiser, May 1937.

132   Cottages in West Street that were demolished in August 1943 for the purpose of extending the premises of the J.L. Jameson Company who were engaged on important war work.

133   The machine shop of the J.L. Jameson Company. They were established in Ewell in 1933 and were there until the early 1960s when they moved to Chessington to a factory they had opened there in about 1950. Their main product was specialised heavy duty machine tools.

one on the north side of Nonsuch Park. Schools, hospitals and factories had to have shelters built.

War Work

Thousands of young men and women joined the forces and left the borough. All able-bodied people were expected to help the war effort. As more and more of our merchant ships were sunk by U-boats, food imports were cut to less than 50 per cent of pre-war levels, and increased home production of food became of vital importance. 'Dig for victory' became the slogan, and people were exhorted to replace the flowers in their gardens by fruit and vegetables and to cultivate allotments. Some 2,300 allotments were made available in the borough on any suitable areas of land not in use. People were encouraged to keep pigs and special arrangements were made to collect waste food for them.

Large areas of land were put under the plough and farmed commercially, with the help of labour provided by 'land girls', members of the Women's Land Army (W.L.A.). Land girls also replaced farm workers who had been 'called-up' on regular farms. Many girls of Epsom and Ewell joined the W.L.A. and some of them worked on local farms and small-holdings. They worked long hours for 42s. per week, which was considerably less than regular farm workers received. At one stage of the war the girls would meet at Epsom Clocktower and be taken by lorry to their places of work.

In 1943 the Surrey War Agricultural Executive proposed that The Hill on Epsom Race Course should be cultivated, but did not press the case in the face of local objections and the unsuitability of the chalk soil. Part of Walton Downs was used. Ashtead and Epsom Commons grew potatoes and corn.

Digging for victory was not the only war effort. Although Epsom and Ewell had no major factories, numerous small 'shadow factories' were set up to manufacture components to feed the large factories making armaments and munitions. A motor service centre at the junction of Ewell Bypass and Reigate Road was converted into a factory to produce gun-sights and munitions after the original factory in Croydon was bombed in August 1940. Jameson's engineering factory in West Street, that had been established in Ewell in 1933, made aero engines and other aircraft components. They employed as many as 180 people. A law passed in May 1943 made part-time war work compulsory even for women of 18 to 45 years old, and some of these worked in the factories.

Rationing

Rationing of food had been introduced in January 1940. Coupons from ration books were needed for foods such as butter, meat, sugar and tea. Although beer was not rationed it was in short supply and heavily taxed. Some alleviation to food rationing was provided by 'British Restaurants' that were set up to provide basic midday meals off the ration. At least four were provided in Epsom and Ewell, including one in the Congregational Church Hall in London Road, Ewell and one in the Church Room of All Saints Church, Fulford Road, Ewell.

The Defence of England

After the dramatic evacuation of British forces from the beaches of Dunkirk in June 1940 a German invasion seemed inevitable and the British prepared to repel all attacks. The Local Defence Volunteers (the L.D.V. or Dad's Army) were formed, taking any man from 17 to 65 not already in the forces. By the end of June 1940 nearly 1,500,000 men had registered, some 1,400 of them in Epsom and Ewell. For uniforms they had arm bands carrying the letters L.D.V. and most of their weapons were privately owned sporting guns supplemented by pitchforks and knives. However, In July

1940 the L.D.V. became the Home Guard and proper uniforms and weapons were gradually made available.

The local battalion of the Home Guard was the 56th Surrey (Epsom and Banstead). They had numerous units in the borough; those in Ewell are thought to have included units located at Ewell Court, The Upper Mill and Jameson's factory in West Street (a factory platoon). Members of the Home Guard from Epsom and Ewell manned four 3.7 inch anti-aircraft guns at Raynes Park. Training was provided by a company of the Welsh Guards that was stationed at Epsom Grandstand and also by Canadian troops. Units of the Home Guard defended the Electricity Power Station then in Depot Road, Epsom and the Gas Works in East Street.

In anticipation of an air-borne invasion, all open spaces were covered with obstacles—trenches, old cars, metalwork—to deter the landing of troop-carrying gliders. Such obstructions were put into place on Epsom Downs and Nonsuch Park. All road signs, railway station names and direction posts were removed so that any invader who did land would not know where he was! Church bells were to be rung only as a warning that the Germans had landed. It was not until April 1943 that it was considered safe to lift the ban, although a victory peal was allowed on 15 November 1942 after the battle of El Alamein. The German invasion was dependent on the destruction of the British Air Force but the heroic young pilots of the R.A.F. in their Spitfires and Hurricanes won the Battle of Britain and Hitler abandoned his plans for the invasion. He turned instead on 22 June 1941 to attack Russia.

Bombing

The aerial bombardment of Britain commenced soon after Dunkirk, building up to a crescendo in the autumn of 1940. Hundreds of German bombers attacked London. Their losses in daylight raids were very high and they resorted to night-time bombing, and these raids continued

134 Jamesons had their own
Home Guard platoon.

135   Members of the SY56 Home Guard outside the Territorial Army H.Q., Ewell, 1941.

136 The Home Guard drilling at Kiln Lane.

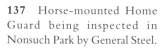

137 Horse-mounted Home Guard being inspected in Nonsuch Park by General Steel.

138 Although in the early days the Home Guard had few real weapons, they were soon provided with armaments, including Vickers machine guns.

with varying degrees of severity until the Allies invaded mainland Europe on 6 June 1944. But two days later the V-1 flying bombs began to fall, soon to be followed by the even more deadly V-2 rocket.

Epsom and Ewell were sufficiently near London to attract bombs, probably something like 2,500 of them, from incendiary bombs and anti-personnel (butterfly) bombs up to large H.E. bombs and parachute mines and finally flying bombs. The borough was spared the rockets, although one did land just outside the boundary near Ashtead Park.

When the bombing was at its height, people would spend many nights sleeping, or trying to sleep, in their Anderson shelters, or in the public shelters. Many Anderson shelters were damp and badly ventilated; they had never been intended for prolonged use. Conditions in the winter were so intolerable that many people preferred to risk dying in their own beds on the ground floor of their houses. This led to the introduction in September 1941 of the Morrison Shelter which was in effect a heavy steel table under which people could shelter in their own homes, on the ground floor, in the expectation that if the house was bombed, they would survive in the ruins until a rescue team could dig them out. They were supplied under much the same conditions as Anderson shelters, except that the earnings threshold was £350 rather than the £250 it had been in 1939—an indication of inflation? Anti-aircraft guns were used against the bombers. There were no permanent gun-sites in Epsom and Ewell but, during the Blitz, mobile gun batteries complete with their sound-location equipment would move in and operate from open areas such as Nonsuch Park. It has been said that the main purpose of anti-aircraft guns was to boost public morale: they were relatively ineffective and far more enemy planes were brought down by our fighters. There were permanent searchlight installations manned by the Royal Artillery in the borough, including one on Priest Hill Fields. There were no barrage

139 National Savings Campaign certificate.

balloons flown over Epsom and Ewell, although, during the V-1 offensive, hundreds of balloons were rushed to the North Downs south of the borough, and brought down a considerable number of doodlebugs.

Civil Defence

The air-raid wardens who yelled 'put out that light' were part of the extensive Air Raid Precautions (A.R.P.) organisation that was already in place at the outbreak of war. It was funded jointly by the borough and Central Government and had a core of paid professionals, organisers and wardens and many more volunteers. At the beginning of the war there were about 140 full-time wardens and some 560 volunteer wardens and messengers in Epsom and Ewell. The wardens worked in teams of eight or so from numerous wardens' posts each set up to serve about 500 inhabitants. These posts could be existing buildings that had been reinforced, or small brick and concrete structures erected on convenient sites. There was a total of 55 wardens' posts in the borough.

140 Bomb damage in Waterloo Road, Epsom, 1941.

The wardens were the front line of the civil defence services. When bombs fell in their area they rendered what immediate help they could and called in the special services as required, the Fire Brigade or the Auxiliary Fire Service, the light or heavy rescue teams and ambulances. They also reported the incident to the Control Centre and in the event of serious damage and casualties an Incident Officer would arrive to take charge. The wardens also co-ordinated the work of the local teams of fire-watchers. Fire-watching duties were compulsory for all adults not on other war work.

It was not only the A.R.P. personnel who helped those who had been bombed. The Women's Voluntary Service (W.V.S.) later the W.R.V.S., supported the A.R.P. by providing mobile canteens and field kitchens as well as catering at the major public air-raid shelters. They also set up rest centres for the bombed-out. Young people's organisations did their bit. Boy Scouts and Girl Guides served as messengers, the Boys Brigade helped with first aid, Army Cadet Forces and the Junior Air Corps including the Women's Corps assisted in numerous ways.

It is not possible to be precise about the number of bombs that fell: there is wide variation in the reports. There could have been as many as 440 H.E. bombs, 40 or so of which failed to explode, and which would have been dealt with by the bomb disposal squads of the Royal Engineers. In instances where it was possible to remove the fuses, the bombs were transported to Hackbridge Marshes, where the explosives were steamed out. Many of the H.E. bombs fell during the night blitzes of 1940-1.

Parachute bombs contained about a ton of explosives and because they exploded on the surface caused more blast damage than a normal bomb. Reports refer to three of these diabolical devices falling on the borough, one near the R.A.C. Country Club, one at World's End and one on Priest Hill Fields. Fortunately, none of them made a direct hit on a building. Reports mention more than 1,500 incendiary bombs, mostly falling during the nights of 1940-1. Every road, factory and office building had a team of 'Fire Watchers' equipped with water buckets, a stirrup pump, a shovel and sandbags to extinguish incendiary bombs. The Germans attempted to deter the 'Fire Watchers' by equipping the bombs with explosive charges.

In addition to the incendiary bombs, which were small, weighing only about one kg. each, there were large oil incendiary bombs that could weigh as much as 250 kg.: about 60 of these have been reported.

The V-1 bombs were known as 'doodle-bugs'. They were pilotless aircraft that carried a warhead of about a ton of explosive. They were launched from bases in the Pas de Calais and were mostly aimed at London, passing over what became known as doodlebug alley. The first doodlebug to fall on Epsom and Ewell landed on 16 June 1944 at Riverholme Drive, West Ewell: it killed three people and injured sixty-two. One that fell on Ashley Court, Epsom on 10 July 1944 killed four and injured fourteen. Records refer to some 30 V-1s falling on the borough.

The V-1 and V-2 bombs were terrifying in different ways: one you knew was coming, the other you did not. With the doodlebug you could hear the pulsating drone as it approached and when the engine cut out you had something like 5 to 15 seconds to pray that it would not fall close enough to blow

141 A.R.P. wardens of Post 21 at Plough Road, West Ewell.

142 National Fire Service personnel holding a hose competition.

143   A victory street party in 1945.

you to bits. The V-2 rocket you could not hear: you could be blown to bits anytime, day or night, without warning.

Forty-three people were killed in air raids in Epsom and Ewell and hundreds were injured. Nearly 200 houses were destroyed and 12,000 were damaged.

Entertainments

In spite of the black-out, the bombing and the hours that people had to devote to activities such as fire-watching in addition to their normal jobs, it was found possible to fit in some entertainments. Cinemas put on films; however, Saturday morning children's programmes were cancelled, although not all children had been evacuated from Epsom and Ewell. There were dances at public halls and some church halls.

And above all there was the radio which was essential for giving news as well as entertainment.

Victory

When the war in Europe came to an end on 8 May 1945 the rejoicing throughout Britain was commensurate with the relief felt after five and a half years of privation and drabness. Epsom and Ewell celebrated with street parties and fireworks. The Second World War finally came to an end on 14 August 1945 when Japan surrendered after the dropping of atomic bombs on Hiroshima and Nagasaki, and the celebrations could be completed. But for many rejoicing was clouded by sorrow for those killed or maimed in air-raids, and the nearly 300 service people who did not return.

Chapter Eighteen

Post-War Ewell

Of the changes in Ewell since 1945, two stand out as having had a considerable impact on the life of the community—the building of Nescot and Bourne Hall Community Centre.

Nescot, Ewell's college of higher and further education

The North East Surrey College of Technology came into being as a result of the Education Act of 1944 which put Surrey County Council under an obligation to provide for technical and other aspects of further education. A new technical college was planned to relieve the pressure on the existing Kingston, Wimbledon and Guildford technical colleges. The County Council bought 80 acres of Priest Hill Farm in Ewell, a farm which reputedly had the largest field in Southern England, so it really could be called a green-field site. Ewell County Technical College, as it was first known, was to offer advanced tuition, primarily in science and building.

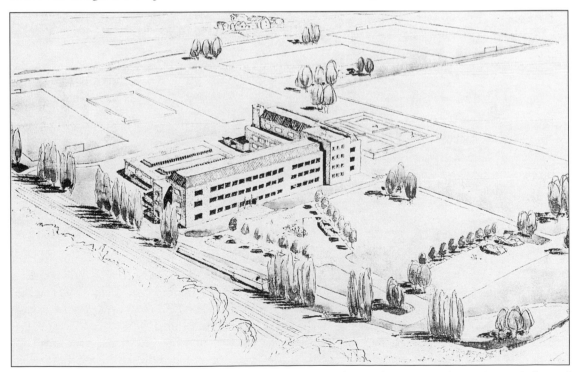

144 Artist's sketch of Ewell Technical College, opened in 1954, later to become North East Surrey College of Technology.

The first sod was cut in a ceremony that took place on 20 September 1951 in the presence, amongst others, of James Chuter Ede, an Epsom and Ewell man who had become Home Secretary, a position he held from 1945-51, and the building was officially opened on 22 March 1954 by Lt. Gen. Sir Ronald M. Weeks. The courses on offer ranged from O and A levels up to degrees in physics, chemistry and other sciences. In the first year there were 187 full time, 348 part time and 552 evening students. Press reports at the time referred to the establishment as 'Surrey's magnificent new technical college at Ewell, the sort of college many students and principals dream about'.

Although college facilities were extended over the years, there were times when they could not keep up with the rising student population and in the 1960s use had to be made of a variety of premises in the area for teaching purposes. Places in Ewell that were involved included Pit House as well as *The Green Man* and the *King William IV* public houses. By 1964 the intake had nearly trebled to a total of more than 3,000 students.

The development of the West Wing of the College included a theatre that was opened on 9 November 1967 by Epsom and Ewell Alderman Adrian Mann, Chairman of the Board of Governors, and was named after him. Enrolments of students for 1998-9 has risen to 2,306 full-time and 5,274 part-time (including evening), with a full-time staff of 420 and part-time staff of approximately 350. The College was offering further education courses in subjects as diverse as art and design, animal care and horticulture and business studies. The degree courses encompass many disciplines, including biology and animal science, civil engineering, business and marketing, computing and IT as well as health and nursing.

Many of the students stay with local families in bed and breakfast accommodation, and so Nescot is clearly playing an important part in the economic and social life of the area.

145 Nescot run a farm for their animal care and horticulture students, on part of what was Priest Hill Farm. This shows it in 1999.

146   Bourne Hall Museum in 1999, at which time there were plans for a new gallery design with the aid of Lottery money.

147   In the spring of 1997 Bourne Hall Lake was lined and restored, using advanced techniques in a joint project by Sutton and East Surrey Water Company in conjunction with Epsom and Ewell Borough Council and the Environment Agency. A fountain was provided.

Bourne Hall

Near the centre of Ewell Village is a large 'island' site enclosed by roads, much of which forms Bourne Hall Gardens and in which stands the Bourne Hall library/community centre in a pleasant setting above a lake. Philip Rowden, a well-to-do vintner, had acquired the site and around 1770 built there a Georgian mansion that later became known as Garbrand Hall. In 1925 it was bought by Miss Margaret Glyn to keep it out of the hands of developers and later sold by her to the Borough Council on terms they considered to be generous. By then the name had been changed to Bourne Hall. It was hoped to put the building to civic use, but excessive deterioration made its restoration and preservation impracticable, and in 1962 it was demolished. In its place was built the present community building with a library, museum, large and small halls and other facilities, to an innovative design by A.G. Sheppard Fidler. The new Bourne Hall opened its doors to the public in 1970 and has become the major social centre of Ewell.

148   Cracknell's, opposite the Dog Gate, was demolished following a disastrous fire in 1980.

The Loss of Old Buildings

Between the wars, much of the building was on what would these days be termed green-field sites not involving the demolition of many old buildings, although some big houses with extensive grounds were replaced by more numerous smaller buildings. It was the 1960s that saw the destruction of many interesting old buildings, including the late 17th-century Ewell House and Carpenter's Bakery in the High Street, a late medieval building that had been a baker's since 1817. The 18th-century Garbrand Hall came down in 1962 while its dairy and brewhouse, known as The Turrets, was demolished in 1967. Nuttalls' grocer's shop in Cheam Road, a 16th-century timber-framed building, disappeared in 1968.

Chapter Nineteen

Some People of Ewell

I cannot claim that this chapter is a comprehensive account of noteworthy people who have lived in Ewell. What I have attempted to do is to present thumbnail accounts of a wide range of people. Given the way in which the population has grown in the past one hundred years, it is not surprising that few of those referred to were born in Ewell. Members of the Glyn family are of course covered in Chapters Four and Eleven.

John Beams, the Shoemaker

John Beams, member of an old established Ewell family, was born in West Street in 1905, his father being Head Gardener at the Kensington and Chelsea Residential Homes, in Fir Tree Road, Ewell, and John went to their school. His grandfather was Jesse Beams, the first Ewell postman. John moved with his family to West Ewell in 1914 and then began to attend the West Street School, which he left at the age of 14 to be apprenticed to Mr. Edward Powley, a shoemaker with a shop in Ewell High Street which later became Lloyds Bank, now offices. However, he continued his education by evening classes five nights a week for two years. He stayed with Powley for 10 years before getting a job as a surgical shoemaker at Horton Psychiatric Hospital at a better wage, and went on to become Head Shoemaker. During the Second World War, Horton was a military and general hospital, but John Beams stayed on until his retirement in 1970—he was then asked to go back for a short period which grew into eight years

by which time he had completed 50 years' service.

Beams had been bell-ringers at St Mary's Ewell as far back as *c*.1850 and John carried on the tradition from the 1920s, for much of the time as Tower Leader, until, at the age of 93, he conceded that he could no longer climb the steep stairs to the belfry, and so ended a record 150 years of ringing by members of the Beams family. As well as ringing bells, John

149 John Beams.

was a Church Council member for some years, and set up and helped to run a wastepaper collection scheme which has raised something like £25,000 for Church funds. Furthermore, for 30 years he arranged an annual outing which took Ewell bell-ringers to ring at churches all over the country, accompanied by many other parishioners.

Phyllis Davies

Phyllis Davies was born at Hampstead in 1904, but moved with her parents to Golders Green some six years later. After attending a dame school she went to Hendon County School where she matriculated. This was followed by several terms at an art studio before she started

150   Phyllis Davies.

a three-year diploma course at the Royal School of Needlework. Having obtained her diploma, she worked for a few years with an embroidery firm. Domestic circumstances made it necessary for her to stay at home for some years, but in 1935 she began to do voluntary work for the Invalid Children's Aid Association. In her leisure time she studied singing, played tennis and belonged to choral societies. In 1940 she joined the staff of the ICAA and served in East London. She moved with her mother to Ewell in 1955, to be nearer her brother who was working as a surgeon at Epsom District Hospital; her mother died the following year.

Phyllis continued to work for the ICAA until her retirement in 1969, but found time to become involved in local activities. The large scale excavations of Nonsuch Palace in 1959 attracted her attention, and she helped there by washing finds. In her own words, 'Archae-ology and local history were an utterly absorbing and abiding interest'; she had become hooked, to the extent that she went to many evening classes to learn more about these subjects. She was a very early member of the society established in 1960 that was to become Nonsuch Antiquarian Society. She took part in nearly all their excavations for some 20 years, as well as working with their Documentary Group, and writing several Occasional papers. After her death in 1985, the Society published in her memory an 'Index to the 1408 Register or Memorial of Ewell' that she had compiled.

Elizabeth Deavin

Elizabeth Deavin started teaching at the age of 22 in the Ewell National School when it was housed in a building in Old Schools Lane. There were something like 100 children who each paid one penny per week. The mistress's salary was £35 per annum plus eight guineas for lodgings. In 1861 the school was trans-ferred to a new building in West Street. The mistress's salary was raised to £40 but the lodgings allowance was discontinued, as the new

151 James Chuter Ede as a young man.

school had a house for the mistress at one end. At the other end was a house for the master.

Miss Deavin taught the girls in the large upstairs room of the West Street School for more than 40 years, retiring in 1902. When she died in 1912 she was buried in the church-yard of the parish church and former pupils contributed to a brass memorial plaque that was put up on the wall of the north aisle of the church.

James Chuter Ede

James Ede, always known as Chuter Ede in recognition of his mother's family name, lived for some years at Tayles Hill House, Ewell, towards the end of his life. He was born in Epsom and from humble beginnings advanced to high office in government and was elevated to the peerage. With the help of scholarships, he became a teacher and taught at a number of Surrey schools.

After sevice in the army in First World War he went into local politics and by 1923 was a County Alderman. His work for Epsom U.D.C. culminated in his being made Charter Mayor when Epsom and Ewell became a borough. His work with Surrey County Council had a big impact on education, health and conservation in the county.

He was elected to Parliament as a Labour M.P. for South Shields in 1929 and except for short periods held that seat until his retirement in 1964. Chuter Ede received his first ministerial appointment in the Second World War as parliamentary secretary in the Ministry of Education, and helped bring the Education Act of 1944 to the Statute Book. In 1945 Clement Attlee appointed him Home Secretary, a position he held until 1951. He was made a life peer in 1964 as Baron Chuter-Ede. He had married Lilian Williams, a fellow member of Surrey County Council, in 1917: they had no children.

Augustus William Gadesden

Augustus William Gadesden, only son of James Gadesden of Ewell Castle, was born in 1816, and inherited the house in 1877. His main business was as a sugar refiner (he owned two refineries in East London), but he was also the principal partner in a large colliery in Yorkshire and a director of the London and Westminster Bank, the New River Company and East London Waterworks. He was for 50 years on the Court of the Goldsmiths' Company and a member of the Building and Finance Committee of the Imperial Institute. Other public appointments included being Chairman of the Banstead Lunatic Asylum, a Justice of the Peace, and High Sheriff for Surrey in 1889. He was a keen gardener and enlarged the grounds of his estate by purchasing neighbouring land.

He married in 1843, his wife dying in 1881, but not before she had given him nine children, eight of whom survived him. After A.W. Gadesden's death in 1901, his heirs sold Ewell Castle.

Henry Kitchen

Henry Kitchen was born in Church Street, Ewell in 1793, son of a Henry Kitchen who was a bricklayer, carpenter and builder as well as the owner of numerous properties in the village. At the age of 17, Henry Junior was apprenticed to the popular and prolific architect, James Wyatt, and in 1813 he set up his own practice. One of his first commissions was the design of Ewell Castle for Thomas Calverley. He also designed the dairy of Garbrand Hall (later Bourne Hall) known as The Turrets, in a similar castellated style to Ewell Castle. It was a style popular with both James Wyatt and his nephew Jeffry Wyatt who was to design Nonsuch Mansion.

In 1816 Henry Kitchen sold off the Ewell properties that he had inherited and emigrated to Australia in the hope of establishing himself there as an architect. He met with strong opposition, particularly from an architect Francis Greenaway, who had been sentenced to death for forgery at Bristol. His sentence was commuted to transportation, and he was shipped out to Australia to superintend the erection of public buildings in Sydney. Against such opposition, Henry Kitchen found it difficult to obtain commissions, and little of his work in Australia has survived; in fact Ewell Castle is probably his most impressive achievement. He died in 1822 after a period of illness: it is possible that he had left England in the hope that the Australian climate would improve an already failing health.

152   Augustus William Gadesden, owner of Ewell Castle from 1877 to 1901.

Percival Perry

Percival Perry, the owner of Ewell Castle from 1917 to 1925, was born in 1878. After a spell in a solicitor's office he went into the motor trade and established the English branch of the Ford Motor Company in 1909. Work in several government departments in the First World War led to a CBE followed by a knighthood. After a split with Henry Ford in 1919 over policy, he set up a large industrial estate at Slough, making use of surplus War Office land and equipment, and this became so profitable that he was able to retire to the Channel Island of Herm in 1925. The removal of his household goods was arranged by Pocock's of Ewell, who forwarded everything in a special train from East Ewell station to Littlehampton for shipment to Herm. In 1928 Henry Ford persuaded Perry to come out of retirement to set up the new Ford factory at Dagenham.

In spite of his many interests, Perry found time to make changes at Ewell Castle, which he renamed 'Ewell Place'. He extended the building to create what is now the assembly hall, and additional bedrooms with en-suite bathrooms. The cowshed and pig stye of the estate farm were improved.

He had a great interest in agriculture, and set up a pioneer farming co-operative at Boreham in Essex, and when he was elevated to the peerage in 1938 it was as Lord Perry of Stock Harvard, the Essex village where he was then living. He worked with the Ministry of Food in the Second World War and died in 1956.

Thomas Pocock

Tom Pocock was born c.1908 and was educated at Ewell Boys School. He then worked with his father, William Pocock, who ran a contractor's business with heavy horses. They traded as T. Pocock, and it is believed that the business was started by the grandfather. According to Gordon Ralph, the Ewell Village blacksmith, who knew Tom Pocock,

153   Percival Perry

he was tall, well-built and rugged looking, with brown hair. He had two younger brothers. Tom and his brother Albert eventually ran the business between them. They gave up the horses and ran a furniture removal firm with lorries until some time in the 1970s.

The business was based in Chessington Road, opposite what is now the Health Centre. There is a block of flats there now. Next to the stables and yard was a pair of houses, in one of which Tom lived. Later he moved to a house he had built in Walnut Fields nearby, on a plot of land owned by the business.

Tom Pocock is of interest to local historians because of reminiscences he wrote in the 1970s covering Ewell and the surrounding area in the period around 1905 to 1940, the earlier ones coming from his father. In his work Tom came into contact with many people and he mentions 270 by name. Although it is unlikely

154   Tom Pocock and his wife Lawne.

155   Mary Wallis.

that his recollections are 100 per cent accurate—reminiscences never are—he clearly had a remarkable memory, and since many of his accounts are confirmed by other records, they can be considered to provide interesting and useful information on a Ewell that is very different from what it is today. Tom died in the 1980s.

Mary Wallis

Mary Wallis was a domestic servant who started work at the age of nine for a Mr. G.B. Stone in Ewell and was able to save enough of her meagre wages to have a small wooden chapel built in West Street in the face of a considerable lack of sympathy from the local establishment. It opened in 1825 and preachers

were found to give regular services. Later, she was a founder member of the Congregational Church that in 1865 was opened in a chapel built in what is now the High Street. Mary Wallis died in 1879 aged 90.

Cloudesley Willis

Cloudesley Willis was born in 1865 in what is now No.9 High Street, Ewell, and which was at that time an ironmonger's shop. His father, Henry, was the son of Henry Willis who had married Elizabeth, daughter of Richard Bliss. The premises had been occupied by members of the Bliss family since at least 1782. At one time there had been a blacksmith's and farrier's at the rear of the shop. Cloudesley became a clerk and left the running of the business to his younger brother, John Ordway Willis. During the First World War he was a part-time secretary to Mr. Henderson, the Ewell miller.

Cloudesley was musical and played the cello, but his over-riding passion was local history: he wrote numerous articles for the Surrey Archaeological Society, of which he became a local secretary and served on its Council. He was a founder member of the Nonsuch Society, which arose from the Nonsuch Park Preservation Committee which was instrumental in saving the park from developers in 1937. He was the Treasurer of the Society for many years. In 1946 he was elected a Fellow of the Society of Antiquaries. He further contributed to local affairs by being a member of Ewell Parish Council. He is best remembered for his book *A Short History of Ewell and Nonsuch*, first published in 1931. Although later research does not always corroborate his conclusions, it contains a great deal of interesting information and anecdotes.

On his death in 1955 at the age of 90, the Nonsuch Society erected a wrought iron gate made by local blacksmith Mr. Gordon Ralph at the Old Church Tower, in memory of Cloudesley Willis.

Hazel Wynn Jones

Hazel Wynn Jones was born Hazel Swift in 1921, the daughter of John Swift who set up a motor service station on Reigate Road Ewell. Her education gave her a good command of French and during the Second World War she worked as a French-speaking cipher officer. Her ambition was to work in the theatre or in films, and when the war ended she was employed as a production secretary with Bernard Miles at the Mermaid Theatre. She moved into films where she became a continuity girl and worked in studios and on location in France, Germany and Italy with some of the great names of the film world, directors such as Howard Hawks, Carol Reed

156   Cloudesley Willis painted by Laird.

157   Hazel Wynn Jones.

and the Boulting brothers, as well as stars that included Gregory Peck, Audrey Hepburn and Laurence Harvey.

In 1964 Hazel joined the Central Office of Information and wrote and directed over a hundred films for overseas television. After her marriage to Stuart Wynn Jones, an artist, poet and designer, she gave up her hectic film work to write a book and found a job in the Ewell area as the principal's secretary at NESCOT and when she left after five years she wrote and had published three crime novels, mainly based on her experiences while filming.

Hazel Wynn Jones was an enthusiastic supporter of local charities and organisations such as Nonsuch Antiquarian Society. She had a lively sense of fun, and it was not inappropriate that at her funeral in 1990 it was pointed out that she would have known that an anagram of funeral is 'real fun'.

Leonard Yates

Leonard Yates was born in Lambeth, but when he was one year old his parents moved to Ewell to escape the Zeppelin air raids. They lived first in a cottage in Mill Lane and later in a cottage on the Kingston Road. It was pulled down when the Rembrandt Cinema was built in 1937. He went to Ewell Boys School in 1931 and on to Wimbledon Technical College where he studied engineering.

Following an apprenticeship with a toolmaking firm in Vauxhall he began work as a toolmaker with the Mollart Precision Engineering Company on the Kingston Bypass.

After his marriage in 1940 the couple lived in a flat in Ewell High Street until about 1949. During the war Leonard served in the factory platoon of the Home Guard, becoming a sergeant. He worked with Mollarts until the factory closed in 1981 and he retired.

In reminiscences some years ago he described his pastimes as a boy in Ewell: bird-nesting, fishing and playing cricket and football on the open fields around the cottages. He helped on local farms and went round with the milkman from Curtis' farm on the milk cart. There were entertainments for schoolchildren at Christmas and other times thanks to the generosity of Sir Arthur Glyn, 'a marvellous old chap'. Leonard's main leisure activity was scouting: he was among the first group of boys in the Second Ewell Scout Group and went on to become District Commissioner for 14 years. In 1976 he was presented with the 'Silver Wolf' award in recognition of services of the most exceptional character in Surrey over many years.' He is still (in 2000) President of the Epsom and Ewell District Scout Council.

158 Leonard Yates.

Appendix

The Old Buildings and Ancient Monuments of Ewell

Ewell Village grew up around the crossroads, the present High Street/Church Street/West Street junction. Development after the First World War and vandalism in the 1960s in the name of progress resulted in the destruction of many interesting old buildings. However, some notable buildings have survived, and the most outstanding of them are listed below and indicated on the map. They include large houses built in Church Street and Spring Street, as well as humble dwellings, such as cottages in Mill Lane and houses in the High Street long used as shops. The oldest building is the 15th-century tower of the old church that was left standing after the new church was built in 1847-8.

Moving away from the village, the most outstanding building is Nonsuch Mansion in Nonsuch Park, which is referred to in Chapter Three. Many of the buildings referred to have been listed as Grade II.

1. The Watch House, late 18th century. One half was used as a temporary prison for wrong-doers, the other half housed the fire-engine which can now be seen in the Museum.
2. No.2 Church Street, late 18th-century house clad in mathematical tiles (brick tiles), i.e tiles intended to imitate bricks.
3. Ballards Garden. 17th-century/late 18th-century house clad in mathematical tiles.
4. Church of St Michael, originally a 19th-century malt house. In the path in front is a huge millstone from the Ewell gunpowder mills.
5a. No. 6 Church Street, Tabards, 17th-century with 18th-century mathematical tiles.
5b. Malt End Cottage. 17th-century with 18th-century mathematical tiles.
6. The Well House. Late 17th-century pair.
7. The Cottage and adjoining house. Early 19th-century, over late 16th-century cellar. Once the *King's Head Inn.*
8. Ewell Castle was the largest house in Ewell, built for Thomas Calverley in 1811 by Henry Kitchen, a local boy. Since 1926 it has been a boys' school.
9. Glyn House. Built by Henry Duesbury in 1839 for Sir George Glyn, with later modifications.
10. 15th-century tower of medieval St Mary's Church otherwise demolished after new church was built.
11. 19th-century barn, once belonging to Rectory Farm, the farmhouse of which was demolished in 1905.
12. St Mary's Church, built in 1847-8 by Henry Clutton in Gothic Revival style. Some of the furnishings and memorials came from the old church.
13. St. Mary's Church Hall, built at the expense of the vicar, John Thornton, in the 1890s.
14. Boarded cottages, one partly dating back to the 16th century.
15. Boarded mid-19th-century cottages.

16. The Upper Mill, built in the 18th-19th centuries, rebuilt more or less as original in *c*.1984.
17. *The Wheatsheaf*, built 1858 on site of earlier beerhouse.
18. Fitznells Manor. Once the manor house of one of the sub-manors of Ewell. Behind the 17th-century gabled façade is part of the 16th-century house. Right-hand block mid-19th-century. Restored and converted to offices 1988, now doctors' surgeries.
19. *Spring Hotel*, an early 19th-century house which had become an inn by *c*.1820.
20. Glyn House Pond, fed by a spring, thought to be the 'crystalline cool bath' with curative powers referred to in 1790.
21. Horse Pond, where horses drank and the wheels of carts were cooled in earlier time.
22. Bourne Hall Lake, fed by springs. Tudor pond enlarged in 19th century. Ornamental 'bridge' at south end was possibly built in the early 19th century.
23. Dipping Place. The Ewell springs were long famous for their purity. The present dipping place was made in 1834 when the road was reconstructed.
24. Bourne Hall Lodge was built in the 1860s.
25. The Dog Gate was built by Thomas Hercey Barritt, owner of Bourne Hall (which he called Garbrand Hall) from 1796 to 1817.
26. Bourne Hall. The present building was completed in 1970 and replaced a mansion built *c*.1770.
27. Chessington House. Late 18th-century with late 19th-century additions.
28a. Spring House. Three-storied, mid-18th-century house clad with mathematical tiles.
28b. Chessington Lodge. Early 19th-century with late 19th-century additions.
29. Wallis House. 17th/18th century.
30. Was Maldwyns, now Pisces, 16th-century building with mathematical tiles added in the 18th century.
31. 11-15 High Street (including north corner of Church Street). Timber-framed buildings with a jettied part dating from the late 16th century and the remainder from the 17th century.
32. No. 9 High Street. 16th-century and later timber-framed building, once an inn.
33. *King William IV* public house (now *The Friend and Firkin*). Early 19th-century.
34. West Street School (no longer used as such) built as National School in 1861.
35. Late 16th-century twin-gabled building now forming part of *Star* public house.

Ancient Monuments

There are three scheduled Ancient Monuments in the borough of Epsom and Ewell and they are all in Ewell.

1. Nonsuch Palace. The site of Henry VIII's palace is in Nonsuch Park and the remains were thoroughly excavated in 1959 in what has been claimed to be the largest archaeological excavation to be carried out in this country in one season: the extensive foundations and cellars were exposed and many interesting artefacts were found. A full account is given in John Dent's book, *The Quest for Nonsuch*, first published in 1962. There is now little to see other than three obelisks that indicate the length of the site.

2. The remains of Nonsuch Palace banqueting house. The banqueting house lay about a quarter of a mile to the south west of the palace. All that can be seen today is the brick-faced retaining wall of the plinth on which the banqueting house was built. It is in the shape of a rectangle (almost a square), with an obtuse angle in the middle of each side and with projecting three-quarter circles at each corner. The brickwork has been restored at various times and stands to a height of between about 76 cm (30 inches) and 135 cm (53 inches)

above ground level. Thorough excavations that were carried out in 1960 revealed foundations and cellars as reported in *The Quest for Nonsuch* by John Dent.

3.   Tower of old church, Ewell. When the new St Mary's Church was built in 1847-8 the old church was demolished, but the tower was left standing to serve as a mortuary chapel. The three-storey tower was built around 1420 of flint and stone arranged in a rough chequer work. There is an early 19th-century brick parapet curving up at the corners with staddle-stones on top. At the south-west corner of the tower is an octagonal stair turret rising above the roof and surmounted by a wrought-iron weather-vane which was added in 1789. On the east side where the nave was a porch has been built. On the west side is a large three-light Perpendicular-style window above a typical 15th-century pointed doorway. The Tower is in the care of the Ewell Tower Preservation Trust.

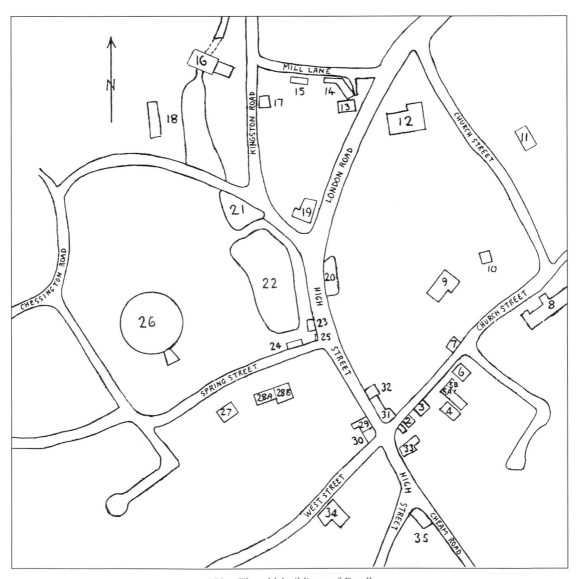

159   The old buildings of Ewell.

Bibliography

Abdy, Charles, *A History of Ewell* (Phillimore, 1992)

Abdy, Charles, *The Glyns of Ewell* (the author, 1994)

Abdy, Charles and Bierton, Graham, 'A Gazetteer of Romano-British Archaeological Sites in Ewell', *Surrey Archaeological Collections*, vol.84 (Surrey Archaeological Society, 1997)

Bainbridge, M.D., 'An Historical Study of the Growth and Development of the North East Surrey College of Technology' (unpublished thesis, 1988)

Blair, John, *Early Medieval Surrey: Landholding, Church and Settlement before 1300* (Alan Sutton Publishing and Surrey Archaeological Society, 1991)

Blatch, Mervyn, *The Churches of Surrey* (Phillimore, 1997)

Brandon, Peter, *A History of Surrey* (Phillimore, 1998)

Burgess, Frank, *Cheam, Belmont and Worcester Park: A Pictorial History* (Phillimore, 1993)

Cockburn, J.S., ed., *Calendar of Assize Records. Home Circuit Indictments. Elizabeth and James I* (HMSO 1980 and 1982)

Davis, M., *Purple Passages: Parkside 1879-1979* (Sidney Press, 1979)

Deedes, C., ed., *Register or Memorial of Ewell* (Mitchell, Hughes & Clarke, 1913)

Dent, John, *The Quest for Nonsuch* (Hutchinson & Co. Ltd., 1970)

Fulford, Roger, *Glyn's 1753-1953. Six Generations in Lombard Street* (Macmillan, 1953)

Holdaway, P., 'The Village Schools in Ewell, Surrey' (unpublished archive copy, 1971)

Jackson, A.A., *Semi-detached London* (Wild Swan Publications Ltd., 1991)

Malden, H.E., ed., *The Victoria History of the County of Surrey* (Archibald Constable and Co., 1902)

Manning, O. and Bray, W., *The History and Antiquities of the County of Surrey* (1804-14)

Marshall, C.F. Dendy, *History of the Southern Railway* (Ian Allan Ltd., 1968)

Meekings, C.A.F. and Shearman, P. ed., *Fitznell's Cartulary* (Surrey Record Society, 1968)

Morris, J., ed., *Domesday Book: Surrey* (Phillimore, 1975)

Nonsuch Antiquarian Society Publications, occasional papers: No. 14 'Caring for the Ewell Poor before 1838'; No. 15 'Ewell Public Houses in History'; No. 16 '19th-Century Boys at School'; No. 21 'Ewell Village Shops'; No. 23 'A History of Bourne Hall'; No. 24 'The Pre-Raphaelites in Ewell and a Missing Masterpiece'; No. 25 'The Lost Farms of Ewell'; No. 27 'A Brief History of Cuddington'; No. 28 'The Administration of Justice in Epsom and Ewell'; No. 29 'Murder and Witchcraft in Seventeenth-Century Ewell'; No. 33 'Victorian Ewell Revealed Through the Census'; No. 34 'The River Hogsmill'; No. 35 'The Listed Buildings and Ancient Monuments of Epsom and Ewell'; A Ewell Walk (leaflet by Ian West)

Orton, Clive, 'Excavations at the King William IV Site, Ewell, 1967-77', *Surrey Archaeological Collections*, vol.84 (Surrey Archaeological Society, 1997)

Parsons, Chris, 'Ewell Castle—a short history' (unpublished archive copy, 1994)

Powell, Dorothy L., *Quarter Sessions records with other records of the Justices of Peace for the County of Surrey* (Surrey Record Society, 1931)

Shearman, P., 'Ewell in 1577', *Surrey Archaeological Collections*, vol.54 (Surrey Archaeological Society, 1955)

Turner, J.T. Howard, *The London, Brighton and South Coast Railway* (Batsford, 1978)

Vine, P.A.L., *London's Lost Route to the Sea* (Middleton Press, 1996)

Walker, M.L., 'The Manor of Batailles and the Family of Saunder in Ewell during the 16th and 17th Centuries', *Surrey Archaeological Collections*, vol. 54 (Surrey Archaeological Society, 1955)

White, Trevor and Harte, Jeremy, *Epsom: A Pictorial History* (Phillimore, 1992)

Willis, Cloudesley S., *A Short History of Ewell and Nonsuch* (Pullingers Ltd., 1931, revised 1948)

Winbolt, S.E., *With a Spade on Stane Street* (Methuen, 1936)

Index

Figures in **bold** refer to illustration page numbers